Mishaps, Miming and Music
True Adventures of TV's No.1 Pop Show

Ian Gittins

Published in 2007 by BBC Books,
an imprint of Ebury Publishing.
A Random House Group Company.

10 9 8 7 6 5 4 3 2 1

The Random House Group Limited Reg. No. 954009

Address for companies within the Random House Group can be found at
www.randomhouse.co.uk

A CIP catalogue record for this book is available from the British Library.

ISBN 978 1 846 07327 4

The Random House Group Limited supports The Forest Stewardship
Council (FSC), the leading international forest certification organisation.
All our titles that are printed on Greenpeace approved FSC certified
paper carry the FSC logo. Our paper procurement policy can be found at
www.rbooks.co.uk/environment.

Commissioning Editor: Lorna Russell
Designer: Jim Lockwood
Picture Researcher: David Cottingham
BBC Picture Researcher: Tariq Hussain
Production Controller: Antony Heller

Colour reproduction by Altaimage
Printed and bound in Italy by Graphicom Srl

To buy books from your favourite authors and register for offers, visit
www.rbooks.co.uk

PICTURE CREDITS

Top of the Pops

Mishaps, Miming and Music
True Adventures of TV's No.1 Pop Show

Ian Gittins

Contents

8

28

86

142

112

32

BANDS WON'T PLAY NO MORE TOO MUCH FIGHTING ON THE DANCE FLOOR

BBC1

7.0 *Colour*
Tomorrow's World
Raymond Baxter, William Woollard and Michael Rodd report the latest efforts of scientists and technologists to improve our life style at home and at work.

Producers ALAN DOBSON
COLIN RIACH, ANDREW WISEMAN
Editor MICHAEL BLAKSTAD
Tomorrow's World 3, £3.50, at bookshops

7.25 *Colour*
Top of the Pops
Discs, stars and the news from this week's Top Thirty
Introduced by Dave Lee Travis
TOP OF THE POPS ORCHESTRA
Musical director JOHNNY PEARSON
PAN'S PEOPLE
Choreography FLICK COLBY
Sound LAURIE TAYLOR
Producer ROBIN NASH

Introduction

On New Year's Day 1964, Jimmy Savile introduced the first episode of *TOTP* from a converted church in Manchester. In July 2006, he turned off the studio lights for the last time at London's Television Centre. In the intervening 42 years, the show became a British institution.

TOTP was Britain's Thursday night fix of pop TV. For eager music fans of the 1960s, 1970s and 1980s, it was the *only* chance to see their pop heroes, whether they were the Rolling Stones, Sandie Shaw, David Bowie, Abba, Duran Duran or the Smiths.

Formulated solely around chart sales, *TOTP* was supremely democratic. Hippies, hipsters, glam rockers, pop tarts, punks and New Romantics all beat a path to the BBC and gave performances that changed the lives of some viewers – and some even formed bands of their own.

TOTP: Mishaps, Miming and Music celebrates the surreal history of *TOTP* via new and gloriously outspoken interviews with scores of the global stars, DJs and also-rans who appeared on the show over the years. From Sir Jimmy Savile to Englebert Humperdinck, Donny Osmond, Noddy Holder and Johnny Marr, this is a behind-the-scenes, back-in-time visit to those battered BBC studios where Top 40 TV Gold was made for more than four decades.

This *TOTP* Top 40 contains riotous tales from a strange, sparkly nether-world of spectacular and ridiculous performances, pop gods, novelty records, drink, drugs, hilarious feuds and unholy alliances. What you saw on your TV screens was only the half of it…

Ian Gittins

'We'll Give It Six Weeks'

The world's longest-running and most iconic TV music show began as a reaction to a thriving series on a rival network.

The BBC had launched a live pop show, *Six-Five Special*, in 1957, but it was off the air by the end of the following year. In 1963, their only music programme was a relatively staid record review show, *Juke Box Jury*, which was regularly trounced in the ratings by ITV's sparkier *Ready Steady Go!*. The Beeb decided to fight back.

'I saw something in a show that merely reflected the biggest selling singles of the day,' said Bill Cotton, the Head of Variety at the BBC. 'It

seemed simple and right.'

Cotton put the former *Juke Box Jury* producer Johnnie Stewart in charge of the new programme. Stewart phoned Jimmy Savile, a charismatic and garrulous dancehall DJ with a Radio Luxembourg show called *The Teen And Twenty Disc Club*, and asked him to host it.

'I suggested we call the new show *The Record Club*,' recalls Savile. 'The BBC didn't like that, so I said, "Goodness gracious me, what about *Top of the Pops?*" They said, "Yes. That. Will. Do."'

> ## 'Everybody's nerves were sticking out like porcupine quills except for mine.'
>
> **Jimmy Savile**

Jagger-ed edge: the Rolling Stones swap tales of Aberystwyth.

kept it all together. He kept popping in and out, going, "All right, boys?"'

The programme ended with newsreel film of the Beatles to illustrate that week's No. 1, 'I Want To Hold Your Hand'. The show was generally thought a success, but nobody was predicting phenomenal longevity – except for its preternaturally prescient presenter.

'As it 'appens, somebody asked me on the first show, "How long do you think this will last for?"' says Jimmy Savile. 'I said, "As long as people buy records, because they will love seeing the artist on telly." And I was dead right, because it lasted 42 years.'

A deeply eccentric Yorkshireman who spoke in jocular riddles and punctuated his speech with bizarre yodels, Savile was not the typical BBC front man. 'He seemed to me to be some kind of 20th-century clown,' mused Cotton. There was some trepidation about him, but Stewart stood firm: 'I thought he was a fun guy.'

Top of the Pops was to run for six weeks and be broadcast live from a BBC studio in a converted church in Dickenson Road, Longsight, Manchester. Stewart and Savile had less than two months to devise the first show.

'Everybody's nerves were sticking out like porcupine quills except for mine,' says Savile, a man rarely lacking in self-belief. 'I had done this kind of show on Radio Luxembourg so it was easy for me to invent *TOTP*.

'Johnnie and I had to guesstimate what would be in the chart in the week when the show started. We got eight out of the Top 10 right, which I thought was terrific.'

The first edition of *Top of the Pops* went out at 6.35pm on New Year's Day, 1964. Chart stars mimed to their singles live in the studio. The Rolling Stones bowled up for the programme in their pink Volkswagen tour van, having played in Aberystwyth the night before.

The Hollies, Dusty Springfield, the Swinging Blue Jeans and the Dave Clark Five completed the line-up. None of them seemed terribly seized by the notion that history was being made.

'I thought *Top of the Pops* was a corny name, not very original,' admits Bobby Elliott of the Hollies. 'It seemed like just another BBC show that would last a few weeks. We were more concerned with our gig later that evening.'

'The crew were tripping over each other,' Keith Richards recalled. 'It was ramshackle, like people were making it up as they went along. Jimmy Savile's energy

The Hollies: '*TOTP*? It will never catch on.'

Beeb Keeps Swinging

Timothy Leary exhorted the flower children to 'tune in, turn on and drop out'. The BBC's lofty intentions were to 'inform, educate and entertain'. In 1960s Britain, *TOTP* strove to carve a path between the Establishment and the counter-culture.

The Who, Jimi Hendrix and Sonny and Cher visited *TOTP*: so did Val Doonican, Des O'Connor and Ken Dodd. Even the location for the chart world's weekly congregation seemed oddly symbolic of the melding of the old and new.

Cilla Black found it extraordinary that *TOTP* was in a church: 'Having been brought up as a Roman Catholic, it seemed like sacrilege.'

'Jimmy Savile was almost like a priest,' muses The Troggs' singer Reg Presley, continuing the religious theme. 'He kept everybody in place.'

Savile, however, was not always around to minister to his flock. Despite *TOTP*'s run being extended indefinitely after good viewing figures for the first two shows, its wobbly-voiced presenter declined to host every programme, fearing of becoming too ubiquitous.

The producer Johnnie Stewart introduced three other DJs who would rotate presentation duties with Savile. Pete Murray, late of *Six-Five Special* and the ITV pop show *Thank Your Lucky Stars*, was initially reluctant when approached.

'At the time, I was intending to go back to my acting career,' he recalls. 'But Johnnie was very persuasive and told me it would probably only last six weeks.'

Stewart also recruited Alan Freeman, an Australian DJ from the BBC Light Programme who was soon nicknamed 'Fluff' for his on-air spoonerisms. Famously, asked to introduce Sounds Orchestral's 1964 hit 'Cast Your Fate To The Wind', he confidently boomed, 'This is "Cast Your Wind To The Fate".'

David Jacobs, a well-spoken former military man and uber-Establishment BBC figure who was then hosting *Juke Box Jury*, completed the team. 'Even on the radio, he sounded as if he was wearing a suit and tie,' notes Cilla Black. Like Murray, Jacobs invariably fronted the show in whistle-and-flute, well-polished shoes 'and maybe occasionally a cardigan'.

Savile, who often sported Dada-esque, zebra-striped, technicolour outfits, took a less conformist view. 'I wore what I used to wear in the dancehalls, which was teenage clothes,' he says, an audacious decision given that, when *TOTP* launched, he was 37 years old.

'I was 20 when I first went on *TOTP* and, to me, Jimmy Savile seemed like an old man even then,' Cilla Black says. 'Mind you, he is like Methuselah now.'

The weekly *TOTP* host sat alongside Samantha Juste, a Mancunian model whose job it was to drop the needle onto the vinyl records the artists were miming to. However, only three of the DJs used the services of this 'putter-onner'.

'The other three lads said that it was difficult to put a record on and talk to the

> ## 'Jimmy Savile seemed like an old man even then. Mind you, he is like Methuselah now.'
>
> **Cilla Black**

Johnnie Stewart was *TOTP*'s 1960s svengali producer.

camera at the same time, but it was a piece of cake for me, because I had been a dancehall DJ all my life,' boasts Savile. 'So I did it myself.'

'I was the *TOTP* disc maid,' says Juste. 'That was how my contract described me. I did four years on the show, then met Mickey Dolenz from the Monkees and married him.'

Mindful of accusations that *TOTP* was too influential on artists' chart fortunes, Stewart established a basic set of rules. Only acts that were heading up the Top 40 were asked on, while no artist could appear on the show two weeks in a row unless they were No. 1. These criteria prevailed for virtually the entire life of the show.

What japes! Samantha Juste and Pete Murray.

TOTP soon became the nucleus of the British music world, as well as attracting visiting acts from America. In its first two years, Chuck Berry, Joan Baez, the Byrds, the Supremes and the Everly Brothers all made the trip to Manchester.

'We loved doing *TOTP* because it meant we were probably going to encounter the Rolling Stones or the Supremes or Roy Orbison,' enthuses Herman's Hermits singer Peter Noone. 'It was an incredible chance to meet your heroes.'

However, many US artists in particular were not around when their songs were topping the chart. Stewart became devilishly inventive, hiring American photographers to shoot them in concert so he could play the film alongside their tune.

For Elvis Presley's 'Crying In The Chapel' in 1965, Stewart superimposed Presley's face on still photos of a

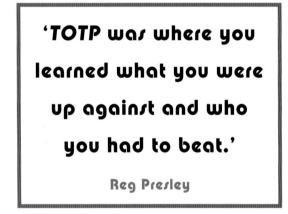

> ### 'TOTP was where you learned what you were up against and who you had to beat.'
>
> Reg Presley

small Manchester chapel. He also hired Pan's People, the legendary dance troupe whose strikingly literal interpretations of hits would fill in when the artist was unavailable.

For most British artists, though, a trip to Manchester became part of the package of having a hit single. '*TOTP* was where you learned what you were up against and who you had to beat,' says Reg Presley. For some ingénues, even the journey up was an adventure.

'I was only 19 the first time I flew up to *TOTP*,' says Colin Blunstone, the singer with the Zombies. 'I sat next to Alan Freeman on the plane. He was perfectly charming, but I was trying not to show I was nervous and hadn't flown before.

'For some reason, I became irrationally obsessed with the idea that, if I pushed on the floor very hard with my feet, the plane would go down. So I sat talking to Alan Freeman and trying to make my feet very light.'

Barefoot diva Sandie Shaw serenades Manchester and the nation with 1965 No. 1 'Long Live Love'.

The Beatles make their sole *TOTP* appearance.

'There was an amazing camaraderie on *TOTP* in those days,' remembers Cliff Richard, and Dickenson Road certainly had its moments. In 1965, George Best was in the studio audience dancing to the Rolling Stones' 'The Last Time'.

'After the show, everybody would bowl down to a club called the Penny Farthing or the Tu'penny Ha'penny, or something like that,' says Reg Presley. 'We'd stay in Manchester and drive back the next day.' In those pre-M6 days, this was a wise strategy, but not everyone could follow it.

'The last plane back to London was at 8.30 so it was a real dash to get to the airport after the show,' recalls Frank Allen of the Searchers. 'We'd have a party on the flight back. PJ Proby was often quite riotous.

'One week Samantha Juste and I had a cab booked to rush us from *TOTP* to the airport and Sandie Shaw asked us to wait for her. Being a devil-may-care diva, she made no attempt to hurry. We sat in the taxi, furious that we would miss the flight, and Sandie eventually swanned out calm as you like, got in by the driver, threw her fur coat over us in the back seat and said, "Look after that for me, will you, darlings?"'

In 1966, the BBC decided to switch the recording of *TOTP* to London, initially at its Lime Grove studio in Shepherd's Bush and then at Television Centre. The show's longest-standing host was put out by this decision.

'Dickenson Road had a real family feeling because the whole building was ours,' says Jimmy Savile. 'On the floor, in the corridors, in the canteen, it was all about *TOTP*.

'There were so many shows being made in London that you would go to the tea bar at break time and be queuing with two gladiators, four nuns and a dragon.'

Nevertheless, the relocation to London opened up a whole new world of celeb-spotting for wide-eyed pop tyros from the provinces. 'We used to love going

> **'Bands on *TOTP* would come to me for advice because I was the King Solomon of pop.'**
>
> **Jimmy Savile**

to the BBC because we'd see newsreaders and actresses we'd only seen on the telly before,' says Bobby Elliott of the Hollies.

'For Northern working-class lads like us, it was a visit to the heart of the Establishment and we felt like it was breaking down barriers. I loved being part of that world.'

Jimmy Savile remained monarch of all he surveyed. 'Bands on *TOTP* would come to me for advice because I was the King Solomon of pop,' he claims, and Englebert Humperdinck supports this sweeping notion.

'Jimmy was ahead of his time,' he says. 'One week, he had tartan hair. I liked how he used to announce me: "Ladies and gentlemen, The Hump."'

Singer-songwriter Donovan also bathed in Savile's wisdom: 'He always seemed crucial to *TOTP*, visually and with that voice: "Now then, guys and gals". I remember once he went into wardrobe before the show and came out wearing a Superman costume.

'I was on the show a lot but I can't remember any of it. The continuity girls would come in and say, "You're on in two minutes", and we would go, "When's that?"'

'You'd get to your dressing room and open up a drawer – "Ooh, look who's

left half a bottle of vodka, or some weed!"' Keith Richards recalls. There were some who found the Rolling Stones – the hippie generation's alpha males – intimidating: 'They seemed scary to us,' confesses Frank Allen. 'Well, except for Bill and Charlie.'

The Beatles made only one live appearance on *TOTP*, in June 1966, witnessed by Peter Noone. 'They were miming to "Paperback Writer" and, for some reason, George Harrison was singing "Frère Jacques" while they were doing it.'

As a live show, *TOTP* was prone to occasional production cock-ups. Having secured a major coup in January 1967 by securing Jimi Hendrix to mime to 'Purple Haze', it took its eye off the ball somewhat.

'I introduced Jimi Hendrix, then started reading a newspaper as the camera switched to him,' recalls Pete Murray. 'Suddenly I looked up and saw myself back on the TV screen and Jimi on the other side of the studio, looking astonished.

'The producers had played the wrong backing track – instead of "Purple Haze", they put on Alan Price's "Simon Smith And The Amazing Dancing Bear".' Hendrix took the error in good part, informing the studio, 'I like the music, man, but I don't know the words.'

After the launch of Radio 1 in 1967, *TOTP* introduced a new platoon of younger, arguably more hip presenters such as Simon Dee, Kenny Everett and Tony Blackburn. Some newer artists also contributed to a notable decline in the standards of studio decorum.

'When Status Quo played *TOTP* in the 1960s, we'd have our road crew standing in front of us, showing us their arses or getting their dicks out,' remembers Francis Rossi. 'They would do anything to try to put us off.'

As 1967's Summer of Love took hold, *TOTP*'s marriage-of-convenience of Establishment and counter-culture looked to be working out remarkably well. For one of its more traditionalist leading lights, however, flower power proved one step too far.

'I decided to come off *TOTP* because the audience in the studio were getting so much younger,' reminisces David Jacobs. 'I was in the wrong place: I had had a lovely time, but I just felt that I was too old and too square.'

The Searchers: 'Get a move on, we'll miss the plane!'

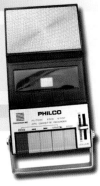

Appointment TV

The *TOTP* ritual began with *Tomorrow's World.* James Burke and Judith Hann would briskly explain the workings of the digital watch or the merits of a car that folded into a suitcase and millions of adolescents would will them to get on with it or, ideally, get lost.

'You'd always sit through the last ten minutes of James Burke going on about something, dying for *TOTP* to come on,' confirms the Smiths' guitarist Johnny Marr. 'It was the primer that you had to go through.'

In 1970s Britain, *TOTP* on Thursday night was the ultimate must-see TV. 'It was like a religious experience,' reckons Def Leppard singer Joe Elliott. Certainly, it was your one chance to see pop music on TV. Missing it was not an option.

'I would be thinking about *TOTP* for three days before it came on, and I would be so excited,' says Squeeze front man Glenn Tilbrook. 'It was such a big deal.'

'There were no video players,' Gary Kemp of Spandau Ballet remembers. 'You'd hear a new song like T. Rex doing

> ## 'I would frantically press Play and Record, then hit Pause whenever the DJs came on.'
>
> ### Glenn Gregory, Heaven 17

"Telegram Sam" and try to remember it. Then the next day, in the school playground, you and your mates would piece the whole song together.'

Noddy Holder spent the 1960s avidly watching *TOTP*: 'The only reason I'd miss it was if I was playing a gig.' In the glam years, he became a Thursday evening TV colossus, leaving him well placed to explain the show's allure.

'*TOTP* was a show that families watched together,' he explains. 'The kids wanted to see new bands like us, or The Sweet. Your mum was into Julio Iglesias. Your dad loved Pan's People, and even Granny might get to watch Des O'Connor or Cilla Black.'

Inevitably, given the programme's musical eclecticism, not everybody in the household would like everything. Perversely, this was part of *TOTP*'s unique appeal.

'It was great when your dad was sitting there saying, "Just look at the state of his hair," or, "What are they dressed like?"' says Noddy. 'You liked that – you didn't want your mum and dad to like your music.'

TOTP was the most glamorous show in Christendom.

At their height in the 1970s, Slade were almost weekly fixtures on *TOTP*.

Even though *Tomorrow's World* had as yet failed to invent video players, resourceful teens strove to prolong the *TOTP* experience. Glenn Gregory, singer with Heaven 17, was one of the thousands of kids crouched by the TV with a cassette recorder and a microphone.

'I would frantically press Play and Record, then hit Pause whenever the DJs came on,' he says. 'Then as soon as the show was over, I'd run straight up to my bedroom and spend the next week playing it back.'

This process could be fraught with peril. One 1970s music fan recalls his younger sister earnestly demanding total silence as she awaited her idol, Little Jimmy Osmond, performing his 1973 No. 1, 'Tweedlee Dee'.

'She had this huge reel-to-reel tape recorder that was nearly the same size as the telly,' he says. 'She pressed Record, the big spools started to whirr round, and Pan's People noisily tap-danced all over the song.'

Numerous bizarre domestic rituals accompanied the sacred weekly broadcast. Home taping had no chance in the many front rooms where the traditional ritual was to cheer or boo every song announced in the chart rundown.

'I did that every week,' says dance music producer William Orbit, who later appeared on the show as Bassomatic. 'I cheered Roxy Music and booed poppy stuff like "Chirpy Chirpy Cheep Cheep". I also booed Slade, because they had taken Jimi Hendrix's sound and made it naff and horrible.'

One 1970s music goliath has very singular memories of the BBC's weekly pop experience. 'I remember how the cameras shot up everybody's nostrils and made it look like you could drive a German tank through them,' muses Meat Loaf. 'For years, I thought all Britons had huge nostrils.'

TOTP's forte was glossy, glamorous performances but the charts were its raison d'être. 'I would write them neatly in an exercise book every Thursday,' confesses Bob Stanley of Britpop synth-poppers St Etienne. 'Then I would write what I thought the chart *should* be.'

Stanley was by no means unique – yet even his pre-teen commitment to *TOTP* and pop music appears positively lightweight compared to that of Clint Boon, the leader of the early-1990s baggy icons Inspiral Carpets.

'I wrote my own chart of my favourite TV programmes in a little book every week,' he says. '*TOTP* was always No. 1 – it never once got knocked off. *Tomorrow's World* was always No. 2. No. 3? *Coronation Street*, I think.'

TOTP was essential viewing partly because it had absolutely no competition. The 1980s singer Betty Boo's love for the show approached the mystical: 'You woke up on a Thursday and it smelled like a *TOTP* day,' she recalls, years later. Yet Boo had a head start on most fans – she was blessed with insider knowledge: 'I grew up in Shepherd's Bush and used to play in the park next to the BBC. Once, when I was about four years old, I saw Mud and Showaddywaddy having a fight.

'Somebody told me there was a secret passage underneath Wood Lane that they used to take the really big superstars in to the show. I think I believed that right up to the time that I played *TOTP* myself.'

'*TOTP* mesmerised me as a kid,' agrees Keith Mullen

of the Liverpool indie-dance band The Farm. 'It seemed a world that was out of reach, all glittery, full of things like Osmondmania. In my head, I can still hear that horsey keyboard noise from "Crazy Horses".'

Nevertheless, kids were used to taking the rough with the smooth. For every visit from Alice Cooper, there would be an anodyne appearance by the Carpenters. For every mercurial Marc Bolan classic, there was an unwanted cameo by Guys n' Dolls.

'You'd sit through Clive Dunn doing "Grandad" in the hope that a Bowie track would come on,' explains Gary Kemp. 'That was how *TOTP* worked, and there was no way round it. You were at the mercy of the show.'

This marriage of the sublime and the ridiculous was *TOTP*'s unique selling point. There was a further dichotomy in the attitudes to the show of the fledgling would-be musicians watching it. Some felt they could no more get on it than fly to the moon.

'I used to dream of one day being on the programme, but it seemed impossible,' says Heaven 17's Gregory. 'I thought you had to go to university to be on *TOTP*.'

Travis singer Fran Healy shared his awe: '*TOTP* was wonderful, but to actually go on there? If you were from working-class Glasgow like me, you might as well want to

> ## 'For years, I thought all Britons had huge nostrils.'
>
> ### Meat Loaf

Cilla gives it a lorra, lorra soul.

'Record and Play': Marc Bolan.

The Sweet were early *TOTP* stalwarts.

be Spiderman. It seemed about as likely.'

Yet other wannabe pop stars were more ambitious. Ian McCulloch, singer with Echo & The Bunnymen, felt his psyche and mental furniture being instantly rearranged in 1972 when he saw David Bowie on *TOTP* singing 'Starman'.

'It was a totally life-changing moment,' he reflects. 'From that day, I just shut myself away with my Bowie and Lou Reed albums and ignored everything else. Nothing else mattered.'

McCulloch wasn't alone in regarding *TOTP* as a weekly crash course in Pop Star Studies. Equally blown away by an adolescent glimpse of Bowie, a diligent Gary Numan analyzed every episode in search of the secrets of success.

'Pause': Guys n' Dolls.

'I studied *TOTP*, and I noticed that some people always looked directly into the camera,' he explains. 'Other people looked at it two or three seconds late, and they always looked clumsy and stupid to me.

'I had my plan for how I would do the show years before I ever got to do it. I practised every little movement of my little finger – the whole thing absolutely obsessed me.'

The luckiest pre-teens had parents who indulged their weekly fix of chart pop. Aged seven, Franz Ferdinand singer Alex Kapranos had a red plastic guitar to silently jam along with as he pogoed around the room. The Bluetones' front man Mark Morriss went a step further.

'My brother and I made guitars out of cardboard with string attached by sellotape at each end,' he recalls. 'It seemed more realistic than a tennis racquet.' Spice Girl Emma Bunton was equally indulged: 'We had sleepovers every Thursday just so we could talk about that night's *TOTP*.'

However, not every household was so accommodating. Baffled by the fantastical sights and jagged riffs of the glam rock years, some parents instigated years of

trauma in their offspring by voting with the off switch after *Tomorrow's World*.

'When I was a girl, *TOTP* was taboo for me because my father wanted me to listen to classical records,' rues singer-songwriter Lynsey de Paul. 'He just didn't approve of pop music at all – he thought it was rubbish.'

Billy Bragg's parents also imposed a *TOTP* fatwa. 'I had to go to Cubs on Thursday nights, so I'd always call at my mate Andy's house ten minutes early to try to catch a glimpse before we went.'

'My parents would try to turn over while I was copying Pan's People and dancing in front of the TV,' shudders Bucks Fizz singer Shelley Preston. 'I used to scream at them: "What are you doing? You are ruining my career!" I used to get *so* uptight.'

> **'My parents would try to turn over while I was copying Pan's People and dancing in front of the TV.'**
>
> **Shelley Preston, Bucks Fizz**

TOTP went beyond mere essential viewing – and not only for the fans. Already major stars by the mid-1970s, US synth-pop duo Sparks would feel bereft if they were not by a TV set on Thursday evening. They even considered extreme remedies.

'We were touring a lot at that time, and if we were on the way to a gig on a Thursday night, we were always seriously tempted to just stop at anyone's house and knock on the door and ask, "Can we watch *TOTP* with you?"' confesses keyboardist Ron Mael.

'We knew more than one-quarter of the population used to watch the show, so the chances were good that whichever door we chose, they would have it on. The only reason we never did it was that we thought it might freak people out.'

Which seems a fairly safe assumption.

Pan's People in another strange sequins of events.

Wham Bam, Thank You Glam!

Look back at photos of 1960s *TOTP* and the images seem to capture a precious innocence. From Herman's Hermits to the Rolling Stones, performers appear framed with a stark, monochrome dignity that evokes a simpler, purer age gone by.

Look back at photos of early 1970s *TOTP* and you could be gawping at shots of the crudest, bawdiest and most sartorially challenged party ever. British pop music has never been so silly, so badly dressed and so much preposterous fun.

TOTP was now in colour in more ways than one.

'We sussed the best way of having an impact on *TOTP* was making the most of our short time,' says Slade singer Noddy Holder. 'We made it total madness so that people couldn't ignore us. That three minutes was our chance.'

Legend has it that glam rock was first invented when a *TOTP* make-up artist playfully stuck a tiny star on Marc Bolan's cheek and sprinkled glitter on his face. T. Rex were certainly the first band who seemed to have been coated in fairy dust.

'When Marc Bolan burst onto the *TOTP* screen he was the first glam rocker, pre-Bowie or anybody,' remembers Cilla Black. 'I just thought, "Oh my God!" He was so gorgeous – he had these fabulous eyes, girly shoes, and all the women wanted to copy his hair.'

Bolan fell to *TOTP* Earth with 1970's 'Ride A White Swan' but it was his return visit with 'Metal Guru' in 1972 that triggered a seismic hormonal surge in one pubescent viewer.

When Bowie draped his arm around Mick Ronson during 'Starman', closet doors swung open across Britain.

All that glitters: T. Rex were the harbingers of the glam rock scene.

'T. Rex were already my favourite group and when I was 11 or 12 and saw them on *TOTP* doing that track, it bordered on the mystical,' marvels Johnny Marr.

'I didn't know what to do, I was in total shock, and I just got on my pushbike and rode and rode until it was dark. I ended up miles away from home, not really knowing where I was, and all my family were really worried about me.'

Bolan's fellow messy beat angel and glam rock progenitor – and, of course, arch-rival – was David Bowie. Having debuted on *TOTP* in a silver catsuit for 'Space Oddity' in 1970, Ziggy Stardust truly grabbed the nation's attention when he flopped a coquettish arm over his guitarist Mick Ronson's shoulders during 'Starman' in 1972.

'The way he looked was astonishing,' says Spandau Ballet's Gary Kemp. 'It was androgynous yet very sexual.

> ## 'Bowie came from a planet I wanted to go to and he set the benchmark for me of what all performance in pop music should be about.'
>
> ### Gary Kemp

The Les Paul round Ronson's neck was sexy, as was the way Bowie draped his painted fingernails around him as he sang the chorus.

'Bowie came from a planet I wanted to go to and he set the benchmark for me of what all performance in pop music should be about. "Starman" seemed like a camp theatrical folk song set in the future. I fell in love with it, and with him, even as a young straight boy.'

Bolan and Bowie appeared alien, unprecedented, *other*. What followed was somewhat less sublime but hugely entertaining, as acts fell over themselves to climb on the glam rock bandwagon and *TOTP* became a fun weekly freak show, a carnival of the absurd.

'We used to get on really well with Bolan,' remembers Noddy Holder. 'He used to tell us in the early days, "You'll never get to No. 1 and knock me off the perch." Eventually

Mud had an idiosyncratic notion of what constituted glamour.

we did, and he was very pissed off about it.'

Slade were the playground bullies of the early 1970s Top 40, obliterating weedier bands beneath their stomping riffs and thuggish swagger. The tartan-suited Noddy, with his asbestos-lagged larynx, Victorian-villain sideburns and mirrored top hat, was a compelling ringleader.

'I got the idea for that hat from seeing Lulu on *TOTP* wearing a sparkly dress,' he says. 'I made it myself – I bought an antique stovepipe hat and some little mirrors and glued them on. It was so heavy that I could only wear it for a few minutes at a time.

'Slade used to buy a lot of our gear from Kensington Market. Freddie Mercury had a stall there. He was a right spieler. He'd tell us, "I'm gonna be a star like you one

The Metal Nun, a.k.a. Slade guitarist Dave Hill.

day." We'd say, "Yeah, yeah, whatever. Pass us that shirt, would you?"'

Yet even Noddy was in frequent danger of being upstaged by his guitarist, Dave Hill, whose absurdist *TOTP* costumes were generally as much of a surprise to his singer as they were to 15 million TV viewers.

'Dave, or H as we called him, would always change in the toilet so we couldn't see him,' Noddy says. 'He'd be in there for hours with the taps running. When the taps went off, I'd know he was ready and I'd say, "OK, H! Reveal!"

'He would come out in these mad costumes and we'd fall about and give them nicknames. One was like a pharaoh's costume with a metal head-dress, so we called that the Metal Nun. Another one was all feathers – that was Foghorn Leghorn.'

It was a mighty long way down from the ethereality of Bolan or Bowie to the shock-rock of Slade. The Sweet, beer boys poured into pink satin trousers and sequined jackets by their svengali producers Chinn and Chapman, also notably failed to produce music of the spheres.

'We were quite *Monty Python* really,' their kohl-eyed guitarist Steve Priest claimed, years later. Yet the rudimentary *TOTP* special effects department served the band well, bestowing on them the cardboard car that drove randomly across the screen during the thumping 'Blockbuster'.

The oafish Mud were glam rock's slapstick wing, inventing a gonzo dance for their 1974 No. 1 'Tiger Feet' and performing the song in fluffy tiger slippers. When they sang 'The Secrets That You Keep' the following year, they stopped performing to have a pretend fight.

> ## 'We started to tone down our image after we saw The Sweet and Slade on the scene. I guess we were being snooty.'
>
> **Bryan Ferry**

Bryan Ferry poses, while Lynsey de Paul balances on an invisible piano stool.

TOTP in the days of Ted Heath and miners' strikes was a visual and variegated feast, but there were times when the music tended towards the raucously samey.

'I remember The Sweet being No. 1 with "Blockbuster" and Bowie No. 2 with "Jean Genie" and it was the same riff,' says Ian McCulloch. 'I loved Bowie, so I assumed that Sweet had stolen it. Now, I wouldn't be so sure.'

While it looked like one big happy fancy-dress family on the screen, beneath the painted smiles inevitably lay snobbery and jealousy. Roxy Music, spiritual and aesthetic brethren of Bolan and Bowie, confessed themselves horrified by the vulgar arrivistes emerging in their wake.

'We started to tone down our image after we saw The Sweet and Slade on the scene,' Bryan Ferry later revealed. 'I guess we were being snooty, because we thought our music was a lot deeper.'

Yet Lynsey de Paul, a diminutive and camp singer-songwriter who fluttered on

Stars on his eyes: the delicate and retiring Roy Wood and Wizzard.

Mael bonding: po-faced Ron and trouserless Russell of Sparks.

the fringes of *TOTP*'s chromatic circus, would have been forgiven for doubting Ferry's claim of musical profundity.

'I had to follow Roxy on *TOTP* and Bryan Ferry wanted to sit at the grand piano but not play it while he was singing, so he said he was going to block the keys,' she recalls. 'I asked him not to as I actually had to play the piano for my song. He promised me that he wouldn't.

'Roxy finished, I went on to do my turn and the keys were jammed solid. We had to stop filming the show, open up the piano, undo all the bolts and pull out the keyboard, and we found loads of newspaper stuffed inside.'

A perky post-modernist who was clearly light years ahead of her time, de Paul even wrote a song dissecting the weekly transvestite carnival that was the BBC's prime pop show.

'"Getting A Drag" was about a girl who found her boyfriend dressed up in her clothes and was angry because he looked better in them than she did,' she

says. 'I sang it on *TOTP* in top hat and tails, with a harpist with angel wings.'

Noddy Holder noted the unions and schisms of the day: 'Mud were always in our dressing room getting pissed, but Bowie and Roxy never were. They kept themselves to themselves – as did Gary Glitter, who invited people into his room so he could hold court.'

'Ah, Gary Glitter,' sighs Richard Fairbrass of Right Said Fred. 'He's been airbrushed out of history now like the Politburo painted people out of old photographs, and rightly so, but he was fantastic on *TOTP* – colourful, and so much fun.'

Elton John entered the 1970s singing backing vocals on *TOTP* for Brotherhood of Man and Pickettywitch. By 1972, he

Before the fall: Gary Glitter was a *TOTP* regular.

was an A-lister modelling a spectacular array of ten-inch platform heels and comedy glasses with battery-powered windscreen wipers.

Alvin Stardust cultivated a huge quiff, wore his rings outside his gloves and pouted like a camp Elvis through hits like 'My Coo-Ca-Choo' and 'Jealous Mind'. *TOTP* proved to be a portal to great things: he went on to be road safety adverts' Green Cross Man.

Perhaps glam's most visually deranged and comedic ambassadors were Wizzard. Fronted by the hirsute and face-painted Roy Wood, a Tolkien hobbit in cheap slap, they were prone to taking to the *TOTP* stage dressed as gorillas or pantomime horses.

'Roy Wood once played an upright Hoover on *TOTP*,' chortles Dave Lee Travis. Wood puzzlingly regarded his burlesque boogie as cathartic: 'I'd shed all my inhibitions on stage then go back to being quiet, like a Jekyll and Hyde thing.' Yet one gobsmacked young viewer was soaking up his pantomime rock.

'Wizzard were the reason that I wanted to be in a band with guitarists dressed as angels on roller skates,' admits Dr & the Medics singer Clive Jackson. 'In the 1980s, we copied them by wearing different costumes and doing something daft every time we went on.'

Glam rock was a uniquely British proposition that never played well in America. Despite this, *TOTP* had its own in-house Yank duo who fitted perfectly into the era's showy, splashy ethos.

When Sparks debuted 'This Town Ain't Big Enough For Both Of Us' in 1972, operatic singer Russell Mael discharged an (unloaded) shotgun at the

> ## 'I scared them so much that they watched Sparks from behind the sofa.'
>
> ### Ron Mael, keyboardist, Sparks

audience as his keyboardist brother, Ron, stared out the camera like a man contemplating annexing Poland.

'A lot of people have told me that, when they were children, I scared them so much that they watched Sparks from behind the sofa,' says Ron Mael. 'I had no idea I was having that effect. I was just trying to be subtle and low-key.

'But *TOTP* was a wonderful programme to appear on in the early 1970s. Pop music was fantastic then, and if you were of an ironic bent, you could go on the show in an ironic way and that was cool too. We were very proud to be part of it.'

Alvin Stardust went from 'My Coo-Ca-Choo' to 'Look right, left, and right again.'

Gonna Make You A Star

At its rambunctious 1970s peak, *TOTP* was ubiquitous and all-powerful. More than 15 million people tuned in every week: individual shows and Christmas specials often nudged 20 million. For the music world's publicity-hungry stars, this was the Promised Land.

'You would sing your hit and 17 or 18 million people would see it,' says Noddy Holder. 'The effect on sales and being recognised in the street the next day was mind-blowing. It was amazing how powerful one pop show could be.

'Even if we were on tour, we'd fly back to do it. Sometimes we'd record a show then fly out to play a gig in Berlin that night. It was worth it.'

'We had it written into our record contract that, if we got offered *TOTP*, we did it, even if we were on tour in the Far East,' says Cheryl Baker of Bucks Fizz. 'If we had a gig arranged for the same night, we didn't play it.'

'One year I had booked a Christmas holiday in America,'

agrees Mike Nolan of the same band. 'When we realised we were doing *TOTP*, I cancelled it. It never even occurred to me not to.'

'It would have been ridiculous to turn down *TOTP*,' says Nicky Stevens of the 1970s easy-listening popsters Brotherhood of Man. 'Once, we were in Cyprus and hired a private jet to fly us back. That was how important it was.'

TOTP was a rewarding but capricious mistress. Artists would normally only learn on a Monday if they were required for that week's show, dependent on their chart position. An appearance was an absolute shoo-in to propel their single further up the chart.

It was a peerless sales and promotion vehicle but *TOTP* had a far greater cultural significance. Part rite of passage and part seal of approval, an invitation to Wood Lane was shorthand for pop success in the British psyche. Put simply, it meant you had arrived. You were a pop star.

> ## 'I used to consider myself a failure until I had been on *TOTP*.'
>
> ### Jarvis Cocker

Bucks Fizz, on the run from the fashion police.

'TOTP had glamour – that thing where the ordinary is made special,' Alex James of Blur has reflected. 'When you told taxi drivers you were in a band, they'd ask you if you had been on TOTP. That was the benchmark.'

Jarvis Cocker had ten years of struggle with Pulp before the band made their Britpop breakthrough and pinpointed the exact juncture where his career took a quantum leap: 'I used to consider myself a failure until I had been on TOTP.'

'I always divide my life into before and after TOTP,' admits Marc Almond of Soft Cell. 'Suddenly I was in everybody's home, all over the country. Overnight, you go from being totally anonymous to every single person recognising you in the street.

'You get very diverse reactions – some people are in awe, some are aggressive. It was a lot to cope with. I couldn't live in Leeds any more – I had to move to London.'

As well as hinting at future platinum record sales, a TOTP appearance served a vital short-term function. A slot on prime-time Thursday night BBC TV was a great way for young artists to reassure their anxious friends and family that they weren't total wasters.

'It showed your parents, teachers and girlfriends that you should be respected,' notes DJ Mike Read. 'It was a major, major thing – you had reached the very pinnacle of British pop.'

'Being on TOTP was a big deal because it was a vindication of the path that you had taken in life,' agrees Wayne Hussey, who was in Dead Or Alive and Sisters of Mercy before finally getting on the show with the late 1980s Goth rockers The Mission.

'It was OK telling your parents that you wanted to be

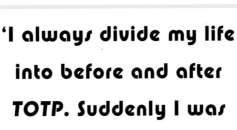

TOTP was a tipping point for Wayne Hussey and The Mission.

a musician, but for a lot of people that meant nothing until you had been on TOTP, even if you were recording albums and playing decent-sized venues. TOTP is what made my relatives finally start taking me seriously.'

For the Manic Street Preachers singer James Dean Bradfield the first time they did TOTP was incredible. 'I just felt like, "Grandma, I'm never going to work again!"'

Way beyond sales figures and astute career moves, getting on TOTP was an exotic, visceral thrill. It was a buzz even if you weren't in the band. Before forming Oasis, Noel Gallagher often roadied for Inspiral Carpets and relished the chance to visit the BBC with them. 'When I was young, I never used to go to gigs or anything like that,' he told Jeff Simpson in the book Top of the Pops: 1964–2002. 'So TOTP was where it all started for me.

> ## 'I always divide my life into before and after TOTP. Suddenly I was in everybody's home.'
>
> Marc Almond, Soft Cell

'I went with the Inspirals and I used to stand somewhere off camera, then go home and watch it, and go, "Look – there's me!" I'd pause the video and say, "You can't actually see me, but you see that shadow? That's me!"'

Some people reach the top and keep climbing. For many frustrated provincial would-be pop stars, an appearance on *TOTP* was the limit of their ambitions. A select few dared to dream of the Holy Grail – being played at 5 to 8pm on Thursday. Getting to No. 1.

'That was the ultimate height of my ambition,' confirms Gary Numan. 'For anybody who wanted to be a pop star,

it was *the* programme to be on – and being No. 1 on *TOTP* was the absolute pinnacle.'

If *TOTP* was an initiation ritual, being No. 1 involved something akin to deification. The most unlikely contenders gained in mystique from being, however temporarily, cock of the walk. That even included Showaddywaddy.

'"Under The Moon Of Love" was No. 1 for three weeks in 1976,' recalls Dave Bartram, the singer with the glam-era rockabilly revivalists. 'The additional respect we got from our contemporaries in that time was amazing.'

Regular chart-toppers Slade bestrode *TOTP* like glittery

Showaddywaddy: who could fail to respect these men?

colossi. Wolverhampton's loudest and lairiest staked out no less than six No. 1s between 1971 and 1973 and bassist Jim Lea admitted to relishing the prestige of being spangly Gods among men.

'I remember going straight in at No. 1 with "Cum On Feel The Noize",' Lea told the *Guardian*. 'We walked into the studio and the other acts went quiet.'

It beamed you into the minds of 15 million pop fans, opened the door to prospective fame and riches, and gave you the thrill of your life. At its quicksilver 1970s zenith, it appeared there was nothing *TOTP* couldn't do. Why, it

> ### 'For anybody who wanted to be a pop star, it was the programme to be on – and being No. 1 on *TOTP* was the absolute pinnacle.'
>
> #### Gary Numan

could even heal broken families.

Having left home to study for a drama degree at Birmingham University in 1978, Simon Le Bon had quit his course to join Duran Duran. Angered by this fecklessness, his dad broke off all contact and the father and son remained estranged until March 1981, when the band debuted on *TOTP* with 'Planet Earth'.

'I heard nothing from my father for a long time,' Le Bon later explained. 'Then we got on *TOTP* and he called me up and just said, "Well, I guess you are doing OK after all then, Simon."'

TOTP gave Slade a platform for success.

BBC
Top of the Pops
DRESSING ROOM 6

Do You Remember The First Time?

On Thursday night TV screens, *TOTP* was an orgiastic festival of excess, a hedonistic carnival of musical abandon framed by fluorescent lighting and twinkling fairy lights and populated by hundreds of sexy, gyrating, beautiful party people.

The reality was different. Every hyperventilating artist who arrived at the BBC to record the show had the same first impression: utter amazement that the poky studio was slightly larger than the average broom cupboard and there were scarcely enough people in the audience to fill the camera lens.

'I couldn't believe how small it was, and how early I had to get there,' says Johnny Marr. 'I'd never imagined Marc Bolan having to get up at 8 in the morning, go to a dingy studio with people still sweeping up from *Blue Peter* the day

before, and sit around for 11 hours.'

'It was exciting being there, but not glamorous,' agrees Andy McCluskey, the singer in Orchestral Manoeuvres In The Dark. 'The stages were held together with gaffer tape and hope and our shoes stuck to them. Those *TOTP* flashing lights got away with murder.'

This shock at the grubby surroundings was fleeting. This was still the BBC, still *TOTP*, the culmination of years of provincial dreaming. Faced with grasping their life's dearest ambition, some first-time visitors went into mental meltdown.

'It just felt so strange, utterly surreal,' admits Keith Mullen of baggy era Liverpool band the Farm. 'I wasn't sure it was really happening.' Clive Jackson, the frontman of Dr & the Medics, felt a similar awed detachment: 'Finding myself in the *TOTP* studio was unreal. It was like meeting Elvis.'

> ## 'The stages were held together with gaffer tape and hope and our shoes stuck to them.'
>
> ### Andy McCluskey, OMD

'Bloody glamorous around here, innit?'

Status Quo, in their soppy clothes.

'We went on in 1993 and it was the most exciting thing that had ever happened to me,' says Bob Stanley of Britpop synth band St Etienne. 'I remember everything about the day vividly.

'I shook hands with Ray from 2 Unlimited and heard Rolf Harris swear, which was quite shocking. He said, "Fuck!" and I thought, "Bloody hell!"'

'I was absolutely petrified,' admits Right Said Fred singer Richard Fairbrass. 'We bumped into David Bowie, whom I knew slightly, in a waiting area before we went in, and it made me realise – I'm on the same show as you! That was very cool.'

'When Soft Cell first went on *TOTP* I was living in a student house in Leeds and took the call on a payphone in the hallway,' remembers Marc Almond.

'We were on between Shakin' Stevens doing "Green Door" and Aneka doing "Japanese Boy". The next week, I took a call on the same phone telling me we were No 1.'

> **'Finding myself in the TOTP studio was unreal. It was like meeting Elvis.'**
>
> **Clive Jackson, Dr & the Medics**

In the late 1960s, gentlemen of a certain age still exercised a correct deference towards the BBC. Francis Rossi remembers Status Quo's manager insisting on an exercise in old-school etiquette when the band arrived at the studio.

'He made us shake hands with all the cameramen,' he says. 'We were just kids with our bouffant hair glued down and parted in the middle, in our soppy clothes, and we went round shaking hands with all these surly old BBC workers who were obviously thinking, "What a bunch of fucking twats."

'But on that first appearance, there was one part of the programme where our drummer caught sight of himself on a monitor and this huge beam just broke out across his face. He couldn't believe he was seeing himself on the telly.'

Far from being intimidated, the secret to a classic first performance was clearly to conquer all inhibitions and *carpe diem*. After scrutinising *TOTP* every Thursday night for

years, Gary Numan arrived on a mission – although he was lucky to be there in the first place.

'I wasn't in the Top 40 but they had a section called "Bubbling Under" where they played a record just outside it,' he recalls. 'They had to choose between Simple Minds and us and they decided that Tubeway Army was a more interesting name than Simple Minds.

'I felt awkward and clumsy and like I didn't belong but I knew *TOTP* was my one big shot, so I just tried to put the fear and nerves to one side and take on the persona of an arrogant person who didn't care, even though inside I was shitting my pants.'

Arriving with a barrage of lighting and camera angle requests for the studio crew, Numan patently took his *TOTP* debut rather more seriously than had glam rock court jesters Mud when they performed 'Crazy' in 1973.

'We all wore different loud suits and I decided that I would play my guitar in the lotus position,' guitarist Rob Davis explained, years later. 'Our drummer, for reasons best known to himself, was doing Groucho Marx impersonations.'

Traditionally, a first *TOTP* appearance was an unmitigated thrill for any nascent artist. Nevertheless, when Blur debuted with the baggy-esque 'There's No Other Way' in 1991, Damon Albarn decided to elevate the experience to the truly cosmic.

'Somebody from the record label gave me an E just before we went on,' he said in the band's biography, *3862 Days*. 'It would have been a fantastic experience anyway, but obviously after the E it looked amazing. Vic Reeves was on the next stage doing this big crooner thing on "Born Free" and suddenly all this glitter fell from the ceiling. It was a really beautiful moment.'

Haircut 100 flirted with missing their first *TOTP* when they spent the morning sitting in their van outside the BBC Theatre further down Wood Lane, wondering why nobody was coming to let them in. Squeeze arranged executive transport to the show but were greeted somewhat abruptly when they arrived.

'I was 19 and got picked up from my bedsit by a chauffeur-driven Bentley,' says singer Glenn Tilbrook. 'The whole band got separate cars to *TOTP*, even though we lived really close to each other in south London.

'We were so excited but my overwhelming memory is the stupid little blond one in Status Quo, Rick Parfitt, coming up to me and saying, "Is this your first time? Just wait till you've been here 20 times, *then* you'll know what it's all about!" I just thought, "Piss off!"'

Keyboardist Jools Holland, for his part, celebrated by painting a Ziggy Stardust stripe on his face for the broadcast. The cameramen only filmed his hands. Next time Squeeze were on, he painted it on his hand. They only showed his face.

Some performers struggled to extricate themselves from the grind of the everyday world before entering Pop Mecca. In 1970, Mungo Jerry were heading for No. 1 with 'In The Summertime', but singer Ray Dorset had to beg his boss for an afternoon off his job at an electronics firm to make the show.

Holly Johnson had even more prosaic concerns when Frankie Goes To Hollywood were poised to explode on *TOTP*. 'I was worried we might get recognised at the dole office,' he has confessed. 'We told the record company, "Look, if we do *TOTP*, you will have to put us on wages – we won't be able to sign on any more."'

Inevitably, many artists' first *TOTP* experience was

> '**I was 19 and got picked up from my bedsit by a chauffeur-driven Bentley.**'
>
> **Glenn Tilbrook, Squeeze**

Beyond the pale: Gary Numan and Tubeway Army.

shaped by the calibre of the stars they encountered there. Colin Gibb, co-vocalist in the Yorkshire comedy rock duo Black Lace, set a new world record for a transit from the sublime to the ridiculous on his first visit in 1979.

'We met Agnetha from Abba,' he remembers. 'She just seemed bigger and more important than everybody else who was in the studio. She nodded hello to me, and I was very excited.

'Showaddywaddy were there as well, and they came over and gave us some advice. They said, "Make sure that your second single sounds exactly like your first."'

The Spice Girls were the tabloid world's hottest property

> **'Marilyn Manson was standing watching us and it made me freak out and forget the words.'**
>
> **Emma Bunton, Spice Girls**

when they made their *TOTP* studio debut with 'Wannabe' in 1995. Despite this, at least one of their number was as discombobulated by the big day as any gauche indie band.

'I thought, "This is it!" Emma Bunton later confessed. 'It was a brilliant experience and it all went really well, except that Marilyn Manson was standing watching us and it made me freak out and forget the words.'

It wasn't just artists who found *TOTP* turning their mental equilibrium into a kaleidoscope. Never exactly a level-headed David Jacobs type, Radio 1 tyro Janice Long entered an altered state when asked to become the first woman to host *TOTP* in 1983.

Haircut 100 nearly missed their TOTP debut.

Squeeze: were these cats really considered cool?

'I was so excited!' she remembers. 'For some reason, I went out and had my hair done like a leopard. They told me to arrive at the studio at four in the afternoon, but I turned up at ten in the morning.

'I had to introduce U2 doing "New Year's Day" and I blurted out this really crap thing: "It must be the luck of the Irish." How fucking embarrassing is that?'

Aware that *TOTP* virgins were prone to debilitating nerves, the more considerate presenters would strive to put them at their ease before the cameras rolled. The show's own Godfather figure, Jimmy Savile, was particularly adept at this skill.

'We got on *TOTP* with "Gangsters" in 1979 and Jimmy Savile came in our dressing room and said, "It's a No. 1 lads! No. 1!"' The Specials' band leader and keyboardist Jerry Dammers later recalled. 'We were saying to him, "Really? Do you think so?" Then five minutes later I was walking down the corridor and I could hear his voice coming out of another dressing room: "It's a No. 1, lads! No. 1!"'

A flamboyant shimmer of febrile poetry, The Smiths'

> '**I waʃ ʃo excited! For ʃome reaʃon, I went out and had my hair done like a leopard.**'
>
> **Janice Long, the firʃt woman to hoʃt TOTP**

1983 swoop through 'This Charming Man' is widely regarded as one of *TOTP*'s most seminal initiations. Yet guitarist Johnny Marr remembers being troubled by a very specific occupational hazard.

'I was wearing moccasins that I used to slip all over the place in, and our gigs were pretty treacherous because Morrissey would swing gladioli around, the petals would come off and the stage would get slippery,' he says.

'The show was going out live and, having waited to be on *TOTP* since I was 11 years old, I was terrified of going for six and ending up flat on my arse. So I stayed absolutely glued to the spot and tried to dance from the neck up.'

Errant flower petals, shoddy studios, minuscule audiences and duplicitous DJs aside, few artists were left disappointed by their *TOTP* debut. They were far more likely to take their leave of the show beset by the nagging thought that it would all be downhill from here.

'I only had one let-down about getting on *TOTP*,' confirms St Etienne's Stanley. 'When it was finished, I thought, "My life is over now – what is there left to aim for?"'

What A Sensation!

Aside from the charmingly certifiable Jimmy Savile, *TOTP*'s 1960s presentational style was relatively formal. Heard now, David Jacobs' clipped vowels bring to mind Harry Enfield's 1950s BBC stereotype, Mr Cholmondeley-Warner; Pete Murray and 'Fluff' Freeman radiated courteous old-school enthusiasm.

This restraint soon perished in the bearpit of 1970s *TOTP*, an orgy of wacky japes, fancy dress, visual gags and 'personality' Radio 1 DJs who were human embodiments of those office signs that scream, 'You Don't Have To Be Mad To Work Here – But It Helps!'

'We DJs were used to being loonies and outrageous on the radio,' chuckles Dave Lee Travis. 'We realised there was no reason we shouldn't be the same on the television.'

'The DJs got 10 million listeners on Radio 1 every day and 18 million viewers when they presented *TOTP*,' says Noddy Holder. 'They were bigger stars than some of the bands.'

'When I hosted the Radio 1 breakfast show, there used to be fans outside Broadcasting House at 6am every day,' remembers Tony Blackburn. 'But that was nothing compared to what it was like when I was presenting *TOTP*.'

If the chart music of the early 1970s was raucous, garish and vulgar, *TOTP*'s hosts rose to the challenge of equalling it. They were unsubtle times and the louder and more flamboyant an act was, the more the DJs loved it.

'My favourite was Slade because they were absolutely ridiculous and fun,' says Blackburn. 'That was what it was all about – the razzmatazz of showbiz.'

These were self-consciously madcap days when *TOTP* hosts treated between-song links as valuable windows for zany self-promotion. Sometimes, even this wasn't enough for them.

'I introduced Queen doing "Seven Seas Of Rhye" and they were a very important band, but I was in one of my moods,' says DLT, ominously. 'As soon as they started miming, I put on a janitor's coat, got a brush, jumped on stage and started sweeping it behind them.

'Brian May was doing a big guitar solo. I picked up the brush like a guitar and walked towards him, and we solo-ed together. That had never been done before with a group like Queen!

'Paper Lace had a song called "The Black-Eyed Boys" about motorbikes, so I introduced it by riding a tiny Japanese monkey bike from the car park into the studio, wearing a silly plastic helmet. When I got to the stage, I let go of the clutch by mistake and drove into a cameraman, ha ha!

'I also jumped on stage and pretended to play the violin with Mud. What else? Once I wore a bowler hat, attached motorcycle indicators to it, and made them flash on and off while I was talking! Yes, we were pretty mad.'

Tony Blackburn's forte was unbridled enthusiasm, typified by his gabbled catchphrase: 'What a sensation!' Noel Edmonds favoured wry puns delivered with an arch smirk. The bling-laden Jimmy Savile was still perfecting his role as the King Solomon of pop.

'Jimmy would come up to us at

Check the threads: Tony Blackburn.

Noel and DLT: does being zany make you hairy?

TOTP and give us his advice,' Jim Lea of Slade told the *Guardian*. 'Once, he told us: "Never forget the tide comes in, and goes out again."'

'Artists on *TOTP* might look at me in my strange gear and think, "Oh, he is wonderful!" surmises Savile, before succumbing to a rare bout of modesty: 'I never forgot they were the talent and we were just presenters.'

Not everybody possessed Savile's philosophical forbearance. Drunk on Thursday night fame and power, some *TOTP* lynchpins were no respecters of artists' egos.

'Mott the Hoople had a hit with "All The Young Dudes",' remembers Tony Blackburn. 'It had a talking bit in the middle

> ## 'Once I wore a bowler hat, attached motorcycle indicators to it, and made them flash on and off while I was talking! Yes, we were pretty mad.'
>
> ### Dave Lee Travis

and we DJs had fun with it on Radio 1, answering it back and sending it up.

'They were on *TOTP* and their singer, Ian Hunter, told me, "I wish you'd stop talking all over our record, it really pisses me off." I said, "OK, don't you worry, I won't play it any more." He apologised at once, but I didn't play it for the next three weeks.'

'I wore a white suit when Roxy Music were on,' recalls DJ David Hamilton. 'Bryan Ferry had a white suit on as well, so I said on air, "We look like a couple of ice-cream salesmen!" I noticed Bryan didn't look very pleased.'

This attention-seeking, nutty-prankster school of television presentation was

'Two 99s and a Cornetto': David Hamilton

not universally popular, especially among *TOTP*'s more serious-minded performers.

'The DJs acted as though they were on the same level as us,' complains Graham Gouldman of 1970s soft rockers 10cc. 'Truth is, had it not been for us artists, they would not even have been there.'

'Actually, 10cc were the only band Noel Edmonds liked,' notes St Etienne's Bob Stanley. 'He would look down his nose, then when 10cc came on, he'd say, "At last, a touch of class."'

TOTP's spectacular audience figures and sky-high profile enabled the DJs to develop lucrative sidelines doing personal appearances and opening supermarkets ('I closed a few personally, ha ha!' quips DLT). Given the show's paltry rate of pay, they may have needed to.

'When *TOTP* was getting 15 million viewers, I would get £85 for hosting it,' recalls David Hamilton. 'On the way home, I'd stop off at the Dun Cow pub in the Old Kent Road, do a disco for 200 people and get paid £400. That always puzzled me.'

The 1980s saw a reduction in the incidents of gurning, costume-sporting DJs looning on stage with the bands (The Smiths would possibly have not taken well to it). Instead, a new producer, Michael Hurll, ramped up *TOTP*'s already nuclear enthusiasm levels.

'I'm pretty hyper anyway, but the director would say, "Can you be even livelier?"' says Janice Long. 'By the end of the show, I would be exhausted.'

'You'd get ten seconds to mention the last record, stamp your personality on the Great British public and plug the next song,' explains Mike Read. 'You had girls hanging off you like limpets, staring at the camera, so all you could do was go, "Ha ha! Great!"'

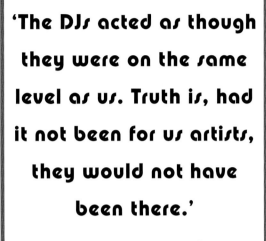

> 'The DJs acted as though they were on the same level as us. Truth is, had it not been for us artists, they would not have been there.'
>
> **Graham Gouldman 10cc**

Deely-boppers were out; Man at C&A was in. Mike Read, Gary Davies and Peter Powell went for the *Miami Vice* look of smart-casual jackets with the sleeves rolled up. Steve Wright did the same, while looking embarrassed to be there in a way you couldn't quite put your finger on.

Julie Burchill described Simon Bates hosting *TOTP* as looking like 'a Conservative councillor supervising a local youth club' and it was strictly sleeves-rolled-down for the booming Simes. 'There again,' notes Janice Long, 'it was always the same beige jacket.'

'Whatever I wore in my early days,' muses David Jensen, 'it wasn't as bad as Mike Read's headbands.'

Nevertheless, while the DJs' sartorial choices would not have had Anna Wintour purring with pleasure, they remained formidably influential figures.

'The Specials were on *TOTP* and we went into the canteen and nobody was talking,' Jerry Dammers was to recall. 'All of the artists were just staring at the ground.

Simon Bates: 'Hmm, that would make a nice "Our Tune".'

Waves singer Katrina Leskanich. 'Then we went on the show and I realised they were full stinky vintage Gorgonzola.'

'The DJs' shtick sort of worked on the telly, but when you were there, watching them from close up, you just thought, "What *are* you doing?"' recalls Ian McCulloch of Echo & the Bunnymen. 'It was like being at a children's party.'

Punk's anti-showbiz subversion and New Wave's knowing irony had fundamentally shifted pop cultural sensibilities. As daft, wisecracking presenters began to appear yesterday's men, *TOTP* producers felt a need for more leftfield and understated hosts.

'Mike Read was sitting on a table with an acoustic guitar, singing "Lucy In The Sky With Diamonds", and nobody dared laugh because he was so powerful. That was one of the most horrendous musical moments of my life.'

Jimmy Somerville was made of sterner stuff. When Steve Wright introduced Bronski Beat as 'a skinhead band' during rehearsal for their *TOTP* debut, he ran over and slapped the Radio 1 man around the legs: 'We're not a skinhead band, you bitch!'

Such direct action remained exceptional. Most artists took the politic route of adopting a rictus smile during the DJs' self-aggrandising patter, then privately unleashing the 'wanker' hand gesture when safely back in the dressing room.

'A lot of them just looked too old and like they shouldn't have been there,' remembers Gary Numan. 'DLT was likeable enough but, well, a bit embarrassing.'

'I always thought they were cheesy,' says Katrina & the

Harry Enfield and Paul Whitehouse's brilliant early 1990s comic creations Smashie and Nicey were to administer the final blow to the veteran Radio 1 DJs. But then something happened that absolutely nobody had expected – people began to miss them.

'Those DJs could be a bit jivey but, to me, they were a great representation of that really showbizzy side that pop has always had,' argues Ron Mael, Sparks keyboardist.

'They had that grinning kind of "always on" energy, a little bit of falseness, and they felt an entirely natural part of the whole *TOTP* system.'

'*TOTP* in those days walked a tightrope between cheesy and genius,' reckons Fran Healy of Travis. 'They were corny, but there was a personality there. The presenters don't have anything nowadays.'

Tony Blackburn, the man whose electric beam became the avatar of the show's glory, glory 1970s heyday, echoes Healy's analysis. Blackburn remains cheerily unrepentant

> ## 'Whatever I wore in my early days, it wasn't as bad as Mike Read's headbands.'
>
> **David Jensen**

about his antics as the life-and-soul of the poptastic *TOTP* party.

'Yes, the way we presented *TOTP* in those days was extremely cheesy and I don't see anything wrong with that,' he says. 'You can only be what you are.

'Paul Whitehouse told me they had based Smashie and Nicey on Alan Freeman and me, and that I was Nicey. I was really pleased, because Noel Edmonds insisted that it was based on DLT and him.

'These days, I tour university student unions, doing live gigs where I come out in a glittery outfit with a medallion

the size of a manhole cover and I send it all up. My first line is always "Pop-a-doodle-doo!" The kids love it.

'At the time it didn't do me much good, because it made the programme controllers see us as old hat. They didn't have a great sense of humour and they just figured that they were employing people who were a bit archaic.

'They wanted to get the new with-it pop kids into *TOTP*, so they went out and did just that. But when they employed them, they soon discovered there was one major problem – they didn't have any personality at all.'

> '**A lot of the DJs just looked too old and like they shouldn't have been there.**'
>
> **Gary Numan**

'No, Tony. We said, "There *are* some nice birds on *TOTP*."'

Solid Gold Industrial Action

In the Britain of Harold Wilson and Edward Heath, trade unions were formidable entities. Senior BBC executives were cowed by the might of the Musicians' Union – and the MU was not keen on Samantha Juste.

From *TOTP*'s inception, the MU had disapproved of the practice of musicians miming to their singles spun by the show's disc maid, feeling union members were being robbed of a chance to earn a fee on live TV.

The MU demanded that all artists should play live, but some ropey performances ensued. In 1967, the BBC and the union reached a bizarre compromise.

'*TOTP* told us we had to go into a studio for three hours the day before a show and re-record the backing track of our song, then mime to it on the programme,' says Graham Gouldman of 10cc.

> ## 'We had to mime "Hey Rock 'n' Roll" in Morecambe and Wise's sitting room in front of their sofa.'
>
> **Dave Bartram, Showaddywaddy**

'An MU man would arrive to check that we were reproducing in one afternoon what had taken us weeks to perfect. It was preposterous.'

Faced with this extraordinary demand, bands did the only thing they could. They cheated.

'We would pretend to play the track, the engineer would pretend to record it, then we would give the MU guy our original tape,' says Gary Kemp. 'It was the great tape swap. Everyone did it.'

'We went to the studio, hung about, the union guy turned up, our manager got him drunk and we all went home,' confirms the Stranglers' Jet Black. 'We never re-recorded a note.'

At the peak of their powers in the 1970s, Abba used the *TOTP* studio time to write new songs, pausing only to go through the motions when the MU rep appeared. Even when the artists got to the BBC, the

Abba: pop superstars or dirty scabs?

unions were on the prowl.

'I was by my drums between rehearsals at *TOTP* and this grumpy bloke said, "Oi! Leave them alone!"' remembers Rat Scabies of The Damned.

'I said, "They're mine, mate," and he said, "No – while they're here, they're ours. Don't touch them."'

'They wouldn't let me move my own keyboard two inches on stage,' says Gary Numan. 'What the fuck was the point?'

With the MU insisting that only musicians who had 're-recorded' each track the day before could appear on *TOTP*, some bands were driven to desperate measures.

'We were doing "Seven Seas" and Will and Les, our guitarist and bassist, couldn't make the show,' says Ian McCulloch, the singer with Echo & the Bunnymen.

'We knew the MU wouldn't let us do it, so we put theatrical fish heads on a couple of our roadies and pretended they were them.'

Remarkably, the *TOTP* charade of sham re-recordings went on for more than 20 years, only ending in the early

Eric and Ernie contemplate the picket line around their flat.

1990s.

However, when Cockney Rebel and Showaddywaddy debuted on the same show in 1974, it wasn't the MU that reduced their appearance to farce.

'The scene shifters' union was on strike and wouldn't let us hump our gear from the van to the studio,' Steve Harley of Cockney Rebel later explained.

'So we ran out, rented different guitars and the whole band mimed playing guitars – even our drummer.'

'Because of the industrial action, we weren't allowed to use our drums or even go on the normal *TOTP* set,' confirms Dave Bartram of Showaddywaddy.

'So we had to mime "Hey Rock 'n' Roll" in Morecambe and Wise's sitting room and do a jive routine with our hands in front of their sofa. It really wasn't how we had imagined our first appearance going.'

Getting the hump: Cockney Rebel's Steve Harley.

Bittersweet Symphony

TOTP had its foibles and follies over the years, but few absurdities can compete with the crashing anachronism that was the *TOTP* Orchestra.

Having condemned bands to spend the day before *TOTP* enacting an elaborate pantomime in recording studios, the Musicians' Union was still suspicious that the show was in some way robbing its members of work.

The MU insisted that solo artists who did not pay royalties to their bands should perform their hits with strings attached. Thus, in 1967 the *TOTP* Orchestra was born, under the benign tutelage of musical director and conductor Johnny Pearson.

Pearson's troupe of jobbing musicians usually covered easy-listening classics on family variety shows. Jimi Hendrix was always going to be a leap.

'I still can't believe *TOTP* made us sing with an orchestra,' says Cliff Richard. 'They had no feel for the tracks. You could tell they didn't even like rock 'n' roll.'

'You suddenly got this very staid BBC orchestra trying to play funk or soul with visiting American superstars,' marvels Noddy Holder. 'It made no sense.

'If a tea break came around during rehearsal, the orchestra would stop playing and walk off even if it was in the middle of a song. The Americans would be like, "Huh?"'

Some took their bemusement further. Arriving to do 'Bridge Over Troubled Water', Simon & Garfunkel were so horrified at the *TOTP* Orchestra's strains that they stormed out of the studio and back to their hotel.

Johnny Pearson's boys were in their element backing Des O'Connor or Matt Monro, less so essaying disco or reggae. In 1977, Althea and Donna grimaced through their slot as the orchestra spectacularly failed to master 'Uptown Top Ranking'.

'Here we go, in a funk-reggae stylee. 1-2-3...'

'Trying to use *TOTP*'s terrible band was a nightmare,' Tina Charles, who enjoyed a string of disco hits in the 1970s, was to tell the website loadofold.com. 'They should have been pensioned off years ago.

'They would be in the pub from one to three, then just come back and read the notes. They couldn't give a shit. Once I had to sing "Dance Little Lady" and it was twice the speed it should be.'

'One problem with the *TOTP* house pit-band was they were all pissed,' agreed Eddie Amoo of the 1970s Liverpool disco group The Real Thing.

'The first time we did "You To Me Are Everything", the producer got drunk and insisted on conducting the orchestra himself.'

Some acts were so appalled by the experience that they conducted an unofficial boycott of the show. Elton John's prolonged late 1970s non-appearance was reputedly largely due to his distaste for the *TOTP* Orchestra.

Similarly loath to re-imagine their baroque No. 1

How can people say the BBC didn't understand rock 'n' roll?

'Bohemian Rhapsody' of 1975 with Johnny Pearson, Queen instead sent a seven-minute video (with typical ingenuity, *TOTP* responded to its length by playing the first half one week and the second half the next).

'Most performers hated singing with the orchestra,' explains Lynsey de Paul. 'I walked out of the show once over them. So did Roberta Flack.

'I was trying to explain a problem to the producer and he said, "This is a television show – the sound doesn't matter." I couldn't believe what I was hearing.'

Johnny Pearson went on to compose the theme tunes to *Mary, Mungo and Midge*, *Captain Pugwash*, *3-2-1* and ITN's *News at Ten*. The *TOTP* Orchestra was finally dropped from the show in 1980, as the result of … a protracted Musicians' Union strike.

Somehow, this appeared entirely appropriate.

> ## 'They would be in the pub from one to three, then just come back and read the notes. They couldn't give a shit.'
>
> ### Tina Charles

Dance Yourself Ditzy

In 1974, Ronnie Barker, in his role as *Porridge's* habitual criminal Norman Stanley Fletcher, was reclining on his top-bunk bed in Slade Prison and mulling aloud over his favourite sex symbols.

'I could call up a couple of birds — those darlings who dance on *TOTP*,' he fantasised. 'What are they called? Pan's People. There's one special one. Beautiful Babs… I don't know what her name is.'

Ask any British male over 40 to identify their most sharply preserved memory of *TOTP*. Some will plump for T. Rex, or David Bowie doing 'Starman'. A few might say Slade, or even Jimmy Savile's tartan hair. The vast majority will choose Pan's People.

In 1966, Flick Colby, a trained ballet dancer from New York, found herself go-go dancing in a Soho nightclub after the BBC show she had been performing on, *The Beat Room*, was axed. Flick assembled a troupe of five girls — Babs Lord, Ruth Pearson, Dee Dee Wilde, Louise Clarke and Andrea 'Andi' Rutherford — and began dancing on Dutch and Belgian TV.

'We wanted to call ourselves Dionysius' Darlings, but it was too hard for the Belgians to pronounce,' says Flick. 'So we became Pan's People.'

'We based ourselves, dare I say it, on the Beatles,' recalls Babs. 'We wanted each member to look different, have their own separate personality, and bring something special to the group.'

Returning to Britain in 1968, Pan's People secured a slot on *TOTP*. Occasionally, the show had used a different dance troupe, The Go-Jo's, but they were only bit-part players.

Pan's People soon found themselves firmly stage centre.

'We would dance to songs in the charts when the artists, who were often American, couldn't make it to play the show,' explains Flick. 'This gave us a major problem.

'We got the chart on Tuesday. *TOTP* was recorded on Wednesday. We had one day to prepare a six-person dance routine to perform on national TV.'

So began a pivotal feature of the Thursday night *TOTP* ritual: the interlude when a salivating DJ would cut to six beautiful, scantily-clad women interpreting a chart hit of the day in a profoundly unique manner.

'Yes, I lusted after Pan's People,' says the US DJ Emperor Rosko, who hosted the show in the mid-1970s. 'Do any of their dance routines stick in my mind? Every Goddamn one!'

The absurdly limited preparation time for each show naturally restricted what Pan's People could do. 'They weren't Broadway-standard routines,' admits Flick, who soon quit dancing with the group to focus on its choreography. 'We were definitely doing watercolours, not oil paintings.'

This was understandable, and forgivable. Far more remarkable was the extraordinary degree of literalness the girls brought to their dance interpretations. *Swan Lake* this wasn't.

Were Pan's People required to re-enact 'Love Grows (Where My Rosemary Goes)', chances are they would seek to embody the concepts of 'love', 'grows', 'where', 'my' 'rosemary' and 'goes'. Only the laws of physics would stop them trying to dance the brackets.

The Go-Jos: predecessors of Pan's People.

Dogs. A dance routine. Live TV. What could possibly go wrong?

So for the Osmonds' 1974 No. 12 'I Can't Stop', four sets of traffic lights hung from the studio ceiling. Pan's People bopped beneath them, showily failing to come to a halt as they turned red every time the word 'stop' was heard.

Boris Pickett and the Crypt Kickers' novelty hit 'Monster Mash' found Pan's attempting to sashay lithely while dressed as werewolves, Frankenstein and King Kong. For Norman Greenbaum's 'Spirit In The Sky', they donned angel wings and fluttered ethereally.

'"The Good, The Bad And The Ugly" was in the chart for so long that we ended up doing four different routines to it,' recalls Babs, with a pained look in her eyes.

'We did it once as cowboys, once as Indians, and I can't remember why, but we did it once in gold body paint. We had an ambulance standing by in case we suffered oxygen starvation.'

'Sometimes, if I didn't like the record, I would send it up,' admits Flick. 'If I figured things were banal, I'd just think, "I'm going to push this as far as I can."'

This was certainly the case in March 1973 when *TOTP* asked Pan's People to dance to 'Get Down', Gilbert O'Sullivan's boogie-woogie love song to his 'bad dog baby'. Flick's live TV routine involved the girls pirouetting around five hounds on stools, one of which then loped off the set.

'I hated those mutts,' she winces now. 'I wanted cute little poodles and ended up with stinky, mangy old dogs that were just useless.'

'We trusted Flick, even though she had a wild imagination,' reflects Babs. 'You couldn't argue with her. We did some routines I thought were absolutely awful, but the only time I flat-out refused was when she wanted us to do a roller-skate number on a live show.'

> **'Yes, I lusted after Pan's People. Do any of their dance routines stick in my mind? Every Goddamn one!'**
>
> Emperor Rosko

Pan's People: 'They were crumpet,' declared the world.

It's hard to overstate the effect that the spectacularly nubile Pan's People had on the UK's pop-loving pubescent males. The national hormonal tsunami probably peaked in July 1975, when they frolicked in bikinis on a studio 'beach' for 'Barbados' by Typically Tropical.

'Sure, we used our sexuality to our advantage,' Flick acknowledges. 'Attractiveness is a commodity in show business. We were very aware of what we had. Personally, I was always flattered to be called a dolly bird.'

Nevertheless, Pan's People made enemies on both society's right and left fringes. 'Mary Whitehouse hated our risqué costumes,' sighs Babs. 'She wanted us banned.' On the rival flank, feminist groups condemned them as a soft porn outfit pandering to male fantasies.

'Ah, but those people never asked Pan's People if they *liked* dancing in provocative gear,' argues Jimmy Savile. 'As it 'appens, Queen Cleopatra wore clobber like that! Do me a favour! Political correctness is a load of crap.'

If Pan's People were fuelling nocturnal fantasies for adolescent males across Britain, it's painful to imagine their effect on the hairy-handed musicians in close proximity to them in the *TOTP* studio.

'I always fancied meeting them but never had the courage to talk to them – they were too glamorous,' admits Peter Noone of Herman's Hermits. 'I was mad for Louise,' groans Francis Rossi. Lieutenant Pigeon's Nigel Fletcher was similarly smitten.

'We stood by their stage during one dress rehearsal, and they were crumpet,' he declares, possibly a stranger to the oeuvre of Andrea Dworkin. 'When some

The choreography was hardly rocket science.

girls put bikinis on, there is something wrong with their knees or ankles, but this lot were bang on.'

'We were always trying our luck with Pan's People and Legs & Co, but we never got anywhere,' regrets Showaddywaddy singer Dave Bartram. 'Mind you, we had more joy with Hot Gossip. *They* were fun-loving girls.'

'Pan's People! My God! They just merge into one hypnotic haze!' enthuses Johnny Marr. Yet, there was one particular Johnny-on-the-spot, Tony Blackburn, who was oddly immune to their charms.

'Pan's People weren't very friendly,' he recalls. 'I got the impression they looked down on us DJs because they were on every week and we weren't. Plus they weren't my type.

'I know they were national heart-throbs, but I had girlfriends who were much nicer. I did make the effort to talk to them a couple of times but I got nothing back, so I just thought, "Stuff it."'

'Oh, the musicians were just like 14-year-old boys, scared to talk to us in case we didn't like them,' says Flick. 'They were simply too nervous to approach six attractive women.

'As for the DJs, they were creepy. They didn't have a clue what they were doing. The only one we sometimes hung out with was Jimmy Savile and I thought he was peculiar.'

'We didn't really notice the effect we were having on the men around us because we were quite innocent and fully focused on our dance routines,' muses the pleasantly ingenuous Babs.

'But I do remember that once Prince Charles visited the *TOTP* studio and we had to hide behind a screen because we were

'The only time I flatout refused was when she wanted us to do a roller-skate number on a live show.'

Babs Lord, Pan's People

told our costumes were too skimpy for him to see. We were dressed as mermaids, in gossamer.'

Andi and Louise left Pan's People in 1972 and 1974 to start families and were replaced by Cherry Gillespie and Sue Menhenick respectively. When Babs quit in 1975 to marry Robert Powell, star of *Jesus of Nazareth*, whom she had met in the BBC bar after an episode of *TOTP*, the writing was on the wall. Pan's People twirled their last in April 1976.

'It was incredibly hard work and we got paid the Equity minimum, £56 per week, but I had a wonderful time on

TOTP,' says Babs, simply. 'Pan's People fulfilled a dream.'

After Pan's People split, Ruth Pearson joined forces with Flick to manage and choreograph their successors. The pair formed Ruby Flipper, a mixed-gender troupe including Cherry and Sue from Pan's People and a black male dancer, Floyd Pearson.

'I was desperate to have different combinations of dancers,' explains Flick. 'The music we had to dance to was so varied and just having six girls was too limited.'

Surviving being *hilariously* introduced by Dave Lee Travis, with a rubber duck hanging around his neck, as Groovy

The mixed-race Ruby Flipper were to fall foul of the BBC.

Ruth recruited Gill Clark, Pauline Peters and Rosie Hetherington to join Ruby Flipper survivors Sue Menhenick, Lulu Cartwright and Patti Hammond. Invited to name the new group, the great British public screwed up its eyes, chewed its pencil and came up with Legs & Co.

'It was annoying to have to go back to an all-girl group, particularly at that time,' admits Flick. '*Saturday Night Fever* was big news, everything was going disco and I really needed men to be able to choreograph properly.'

Nevertheless, as was her wont, Flick made the best of things. Legs & Co were early entrants into the punk arena, although Johnny Rotten may well have stared askance at the girls resembling new wave harlequins for the Sex

Kipper, Ruby Flipper had their moments. For David Bowie's 'TVC15' they did gawky forward rolls in front of a bank of TVs. Flick's fingerprints were all over the routine to Wings' 'Let 'Em In', which saw them letting each other in and out of doors on stage.

Yet they were to be short-lived. 'Bill Cotton called me in to the BBC and said the British public didn't want to see black men dancing with white women,' says Flick. 'I argued, but he told me to form another all-girl group or I was out.'

Having secured – with cosmic levels of irony – a job for Floyd on *The Black and White Minstrel Show*, Flick and

> **'Once Prince Charles visited the *TOTP* studio and we had to hide behind a screen because we were told our costumes were too skimpy for him to see.'**
>
> **Babs, Pan's People**

Legs & Co: more Ann Summers than Donna Summer.

Pistols' 'Pretty Vacant' and pogoing in green lycra shorts to 'Silly Thing'.

Flick dreamed up more routines whose clunky literalness bordered on postmodernist genius. For Donna Summer's 1978 'Rumour Has It', Legs & Co dressed like Mrs Mops and gossiped across a fence separating *Coronation Street*-style terraced backyards.

They returned to Summer's output later that year, magnificently incorporating both a cake and rain into their reading of 'Macarthur Park', while Eruption's

'I Can't Stand The Rain' saw them splashing through puddles in see-through plastic macs, bikinis and red wellies.

> **'One week you were wearing sequins, fake fur and diamonds. The next week you were dressed as a Smurf.'**
>
> **Sue Menhenick, Pan's People**

'One week you were wearing sequins, fake fur and diamonds,' a stoical Sue Menhenick reflected. 'The next week you were dressed as a Smurf, or running round with a loaf of French bread in your hand.'

Yet even Sue must have blanched at Flick's seminal routine for 'Born To Be Alive', a disco anthem by 1979 one-hit-wonder Patrick Hernandez. Obscured by soap bubbles,

Who could ever say Legs & Co were too literal?

Legs & Co boogied then *crawled* around stage in silver nappies and baby bonnets.

Legs & Co went out at the top in late 1981, cutting a farewell rug to the Tweets' 'Birdie Song'. Flick, for her part, felt her second all-girl creation never quite received the public approbation they craved.

'They were a much more slick operation than Pan's People,' she reflects. 'I was older than them and knew what I was doing more, and they never partied like Pan's sometimes did.

'I felt sorry for them because they were good dancers but they never got the affection that Pan's People got. Nobody ever wanted them in quite the same way. There is nothing better than being first.'

Flick had one last throw of the dice yet. The BBC had been incubating more progressive attitudes since Ruby Flipper, and Flick took advantage of this when she formed her final group.

She firmly told *TOTP*, 'I just can't stand this six-girl thing any more. I've got to have men! Some songs need two dancers and some need twelve!' Thankfully, this time around they listened and she formed Zoo.

'I hired professional dance people for Zoo and I also hired jugglers. It was a lot more freeform

and a lot more fun.'

Not dissimilar to Arlene Phillips' risqué dance troupe Hot Gossip, who were raising eyebrows on Kenny Everett's ITV show, Zoo were a movable feast of 20 or so dancers who appeared irregularly on *TOTP*.

Flick's creative vision remained intact. For Mike Post's 'Theme From *Hill Street Blues*', Zoo crept around the studio in detective-style trenchcoats.

Yet this was the end of an era. Video may not have killed the radio star but it mortally wounded the dancing girls. With record companies falling over themselves to give *TOTP* promotional videos to show for free, they were surplus to requirement.

After 15 years in which Flick Colby had helped to nurture *TOTP*'s very soul and, along the way, given the British male more cheap thrills than Paul Raymond, she quit the show knowing she had left a truly singular body of work behind her.

'I remembered getting a mini cab from my apartment to go to the BBC on my very first day and thinking, "I'm going to have the most fun of all my life",' she concludes. 'And do you know what? I absolutely did.'

Animal magic: Flick
Colby's parting shot, Zoo.

The Killing Of Georgie Fame

In 1975, life was good for 'Diddy' David Hamilton. The amiable DJ was hosting Radio 1's drivetime show of chart hits and oldies plus working as an on-screen continuity announcer at the BBC's London rival, Thames TV. Yet he felt there was something missing.

'I had always wanted to present *TOTP*,' he reflects. 'The Radio 1 DJs all did it and it looked great fun, but the BBC wouldn't let me do their TV shows while I was also on commercial telly. So I left Thames TV purely so that I could host *TOTP*.'

The BBC added Hamilton to *TOTP*'s presentational roster and he happily took turns with Noel, Tony and DLT in the late glam years, introducing musical goliaths such as Chicory Tip, Kenny and Pilot. They were heady days and he took his responsibilities seriously.

'I was very professional and had a rule never to drink before a show,' he says. 'I would often go to the BBC restaurant before *TOTP* and have lunch with artists like Cliff Richard or record-label pluggers, but it was strictly orange juice for me.

'*TOTP* was on a very tight schedule and mistakes were expensive so it helped that I hardly ever fluffed or had to do re-takes. I had a good reputation. They used to call me One-Take Hamilton, and I was proud of that.'

In September 1976, Hamilton had a pre-*TOTP* lunch with a gaggle of record

One-take Hamilton fails the acid test.

pluggers, including one renowned as a notorious prankster. The lively meal passed without incident except for the usual banter and the DJ proceeded to the studio, where he initially introduced that week's array of acts with his usual élan.

'It was all going fine until the end of the show, when I had to introduce Rod Stewart singing "The Killing Of Georgie,"' he remembers. 'The camera came to me, the light came on, and I said, "Now on *TOTP*, this is Rod Stewart and 'The Killing Of Georgie Fame'."'

The shooting was halted and the show's puzzled producer took Hamilton to one side: 'It's not Georgie Fame, it's "The Killing Of Georgie".' Hamilton said, 'Yeah, I know. Did I say Georgie Fame? I'm so sorry.'' The cameras rolled again, and One-Take Hamilton did it again: 'This is Rod Stewart on *TOTP* and "The Killing Of Georgie Fame".'

'There was a long pause while big discussions went on between the floor and the control room,' he remembers.

'Everybody was pointing at me. I felt stupid and very strange; my thoughts were all over the place. I couldn't get my head around what was going on.'

Hamilton got it right at the third attempt but valuable time and tape had been wasted and his reputation was sullied. His *TOTP* career was over: he was never asked to host the show again. He remained utterly mortified by the incident until a chance encounter two years later. 'I bumped into one of the record pluggers. He said to me, "Do you remember that day on *TOTP* when you kept going on about Georgie Fame?" I said, "Yes, of course!" and he told me, "We spiked your drink, mate! We slipped you a Mickey Finn!"'

Remarkably, 'Diddy' David Hamilton, Radio 1's house-wives'-choice DJ, had unwittingly experienced a long, strange LSD trip in front of the *TOTP* cameras. Two years later, he was once again working as a continuity announcer on Thames TV. Georgie Fame is a fickle mistress.

Rod Stewart failed to bump off Georgie Fame (above), despite the best druggy efforts of David Hamilton.

Hello, Mum!

In the 1960s, the *TOTP* studio audience looked like moody extras from *Alfie*. In the 1970s, they resembled Richard O'Sullivan and Paula Wilcox in *Man About The House*. In the 1980s, it was big hair and shoulder pads a-go-go à la *Dynasty* or *Dallas*. Yet one thing remained consistent down the years.

'The audience could never really dance,' remembers Lynsey de Paul. 'They were so tame. My overall memory is of them looking uncomfortable and shifting from foot to foot.'

Possibly mindful of this innate British inability to cut a rug, Jimmy Savile had launched *TOTP* insisting that the audience be encouraged to dance by being rewarded with airtime.

TOTP girls were always dancing around invisible handbags.

'I said to Johnnie Stewart, "Mark my words, the audience will be as important as the groups,"' he says. 'I made sure the audience got as much camera coverage as the groups did.'

From the outset, kids were desperate to get on *TOTP*. 'We had a waiting list of one million people in Manchester,' claims the ever-understated Savile, who launched a further incentive for any studio wallflowers to get up and boogie.

'I invented a competition for the best dancer and best-dressed person in the audience,' he explains. 'They weren't *on* the programme; they were *part of* the programme.'

'If kids came along who were smartly dressed and fashion-conscious, we immediately gave them tickets to the next week's show,' confirms Tony Blackburn. 'That was important.'

Whoever said *TOTP* was a meat market?

Some hip young things boogie down. Plus Jimmy Savile.

In the late 1960s, fashion designers like Mary Quant reportedly infiltrated her models into the painfully hip show's audience. Presenter Pete Murray got a request via a rather more direct route.

'An attractive lady stopped me in the street and asked for two tickets,' he recalls. 'I said it was quite difficult, and she said, "Look, I'm a prostitute, and I'll give you a freebie if you get me the tickets."'

You might have needed a golden ticket to get into *TOTP* but the holders were hardly treated like royalty. The experience of one 16-year-old schoolgirl Diane White, who visited the show in 1970, was typical.

'I was so excited,' she recalls. 'I wore green knitted hot pants I had bought in a boutique in Ruislip. They had a matching top but I didn't want to wear that so I wore a multi-coloured thing with big, loose sleeves. Oh, and knee-length platform boots in purple suede.

'We went on the tube, talking very loudly about how we were going to *TOTP*, and hung around outside the BBC for hours before they would let us in. I was expecting it to be like a concert with hundreds of people, but there were about 40 of us in this really small, tacky studio.

'We were shoved and herded about between three stages. Slade were the main act and gave it their all, and Labi Siffre sat on a stool looking very inanimate. Pan's People had to do their bit four or five times and we had to keep applauding them.

'The next night I saw myself on TV dancing badly. It was years before video recorders, so a friend took photos of the TV screen for me. They didn't come out very well.'

In 1973, a 15-year-old Jools Holland attended *TOTP* but did not find its requirements entirely to his liking.

'I was a bus greeter, which was like a biker who wore all the gear that a motorcyclist had, the leather jacket and studs, but didn't actually have a bike, so went everywhere on the bus,' he explains.

> **'The audience could never really dance. My overall memory is of them looking uncomfortable and shifting from foot to foot.'**
>
> **Lynsey de Paul**

A TOTP audience. Note heavy predominance of females.

'No. I was Dawn singing 'Tie A Yellow Ribbon Round The Ole Oak Tree' and the floor manager told everyone to skip around waving yellow ribbons about.

'Well, I was a bus greeter and didn't want to skip around waving a yellow ribbon, so I sat there looking grumpy. They told me I would get kicked out if I didn't dance, so I had to have a little skip.'

The *TOTP* studio staff's brusque treatment of The Kids became legendary. Many visiting artists rubbed their eyes in amazement at what their fans had to go through.

'There was a really camp warm-up bloke trying to get them excited about some band from Doncaster that nobody had heard of,' says Clint Boon of Inspiral Carpets. 'Then the floor managers just shepherded – no, bullied – them around the room: "Stand here! And dance!"'

'We were on with Simon Bates and he never stopped shouting at the kids in the audience,' remembers Glenn

Gregory of Heaven 17. 'He was like a bloody teacher, yelling, "Shut up! Move over! Clap!" I just thought, "Calm down, mate! That's a bit rude!"'

'There were only about 30 people in the audience and they were herded around as if there were a couple of collie dogs at work,' recalls Richard Fairbrass of Right Said Fred. 'I was almost expecting to see an old guy whistling in the corner.'

In the 1980s, *TOTP*'s producers put professional dancers in the audience to act as 'cheerleaders' and get the party started, a decision that 54-year-old teenager Jimmy Savile felt damaged the vibe of the show.

'The crowd were hyped up enough just by being there, they didn't need to be told, "Shout now!" or, "Dance or you're out!"' he complains. 'It made the show look like an American political convention.'

The lapels were wide, and so were the smiles.

And yet the show often featured artists that even Fred Astaire and Ginger Rogers with a gun to their heads would have been hard pushed to bust a move to. 'Mull of Kintyre', anyone? Laurie Anderson's 'O Superman'?

'It was impossible to dance to any Hollies track,' admits the band's Bobby Elliott. 'The audience would just saunter around.'

'I used to watch the kids in the studio trying to dance to "Mouldy Old Dough",' remembers Nigel Fletcher of Lieutenant Pigeon. 'How did they do it? I couldn't begin to describe it.'

For the more confident audience members, the ultimate goal was to stand grinning and waving to their mum beside the host DJ as he linked between acts. Jimmy Savile and Dave Lee Travis were in the habit of requesting on-screen pecks on the cheek from the gaggle of girls around them.

David Jensen engaged one audience member in impromptu conversation on a live show and promptly regretted this rash decision.

'I had to introduce Hot Chocolate and unwisely said

to the girl next to me, "Hot Chocolate are next – I bet you're looking forward to that!"' he recalls. 'She said, "Not really, I can't stand them." I looked across the studio and Hot Chocolate were all staring at me with raised eyebrows.'

Ultimately for the studio pop kids, *TOTP* was only as good as the acts who were on, and that was an absolute lottery. A teenage Zoë Ball secured tickets to the show in the mid-1980s but was bitterly disappointed by what she found there.

'We were really annoyed because there was nobody cool on,' she recalled later. 'It was Dr & the Medics and a video of Peter Gabriel. I wore a bangle on my wrist so that I would be able to see my arm moving around on TV.'

Yet if the artists could under-perform, so could the audience. A decade later, Ball became a regular host of post-Britpop *TOTP* and found herself in despair at the aesthetic sensibilities of The Kids Today.

'The audience were all 18,' she noted. 'A boy band would come on and they would all go absolutely mad. Then we would have something really good, like Lou Reed or Blur or Pulp or Underworld, and they would all gaze around and wait for the next dancing boys.

'Sometimes, I just wanted to slap them.'

> ## 'I used to watch the kids trying to dance to "Mouldy Old Dough". I couldn't begin to describe it.'
>
> **Nigel Fletcher, Lieutenant Pigeon**

Hysteria!

With its stroboscopic lights, breathless DJs and preening artists, *TOTP* unfolded each week at a constant temperature of fever pitch. It is hardly a surprise that this air of simmering hysteria frequently spread from the BBC's studios to the streets outside.

As *TOTP* was filmed every Wednesday for its Thursday broadcast, hordes of screaming girls in Wood Lane, outside Television Centre, became a regular sight. Yet it had all started years earlier, outside the ex-church in Manchester.

'Manchester Police tried to guarantee our safety but even they couldn't stop the clothes being ripped off us,'

says Jimmy Savile. 'I would wear clothes that I didn't mind losing.

'Once I was in the gents having a slash, and I heard a girl's voice say, "Look, there's Jimmy Savile!" The fans outside had drilled a hole right through the thick brick wall.'

'We once arrived at Dickenson Road in our Humber Super Snipe and ran for it through the crowds at the front door,' recalls Tremeloes singer Brian Poole.

'I was wearing this lovely thin blue leather coat and

somebody yanked the collar and all of the buttons came shooting off. I was so annoyed. Our fan club was getting phone calls for weeks from people boasting they had a bit of that coat.'

'Young girls were always propositioning Harry, my elderly Manchester driver, in exchange for tickets for the show,' says Pete Murray. 'Did he ever accept? I sincerely hope not!'

After the show moved to London, fan fever prevented the Beatles appearing on *TOTP* more than once as BBC security felt unable to deal with the demands of Beatlemania. Instead, the band made secret trips to other BBC studios to record live footage for the show.

The Rolling Stones were more frequent 1960s visitors, but the feral nature of the adulation for them gave rise to

Cliff Richard used to whip up quite a frenzy, you know.

some highly innovative entrance and exit strategies. 'Once we had to hide the Stones in bins in the back of a refuse truck,' recounts Jimmy Savile.

'We would pull up in a car outside *TOTP* and people would thump the roof and bang the windows and scream my name and want autographs,' says Cliff Richard. 'It was absolutely fantastic.

'It was sometimes hard getting in and out of the building but it was our job as pop stars to whip up as much frenzy as we could about ourselves, so we could hardly complain about having to get past that frenzy into the studio.'

'I was always friendly to the police going in,' says

Despite their success, the Osmonds could only afford a black-and-white set.

> ## 'Rick [Parfitt] always tried to get mobbed. We used to leave TOTP really slowly.'
>
> Francis Rossi, Status Quo

Englebert Humperdinck, 'because I knew I might need them to help me get out again.'

'We were at *TOTP* with T. Rex once and our drummer, Don Powell, had parked his white Bentley next to Marc Bolan's white Bentley,' remembers Noddy Holder. 'We all left together by the back door. There were hundreds of fans waiting there.

'We made a run for it, jumped in the car and slammed the doors, then looked out to see Bolan banging on the window. We had jumped in his motor by mistake and locked him out. The kids tore him to pieces – scratched his shirt off his back and ripped ringlets out of his hair.'

'Rick [Parfitt] always tried to get mobbed,' Francis Rossi of Status Quo claims. 'We used to leave *TOTP* really slowly. Girls used to write things about me on the side of our van and Rick got so jealous that he snuck out one night and wrote things about himself on there.'

In 1972, American singing family, the Osmonds, were pop's biggest sensation and 14-year-old Donny was the brightest star of all. Yet his desperately dedicated fans meant he could never truly enjoy the *TOTP* experience.

'I'd get whisked in a secret door, do my routine onstage and get the heck out of there,' he says. 'Our security isolated me so much that I never actually got to meet anybody.

'But it was a rush being 14 and having thousands of girls screaming at me. I remember the first time I sang on *TOTP*

with my sister Marie. The kids didn't scream and I realised I had to share the limelight and wasn't a teen idol any more. Did I mind that? Yes!'

However, it was not Osmondmania that succeeded in overwhelming Television Centre but the mid-1970s Tartan Army that followed the Bay City Rollers.

'Nobody could get in or out,' remembers Jimmy Savile. 'There were people from these great programmes, current affairs shows like *Panorama*, trapped by screaming dervishes

> **'I'd get whisked in a secret door, do my routine onstage and get the heck out of there.'**
>
> Donny Osmond

Bay City Rollers: too sexy for Television Centre.

Bros: even more alluring than the Proclaimers?

at every gate. The BBC put out a diktat that we couldn't have *that kind of group* in Television Centre again.'

The Bay City Rollers were thereafter made to shoot their appearances in secret with no audience, as had the Beatles. The ban also applied to David Cassidy. Some of the more flexible groupies simply located other targets for their unbridled lust.

'I finished hosting *TOTP* once and went outside to my Rolls-Royce and there was a very attractive girl standing next to it,' says David Hamilton. 'She asked me, "Are you David Hamilton?" I said, "Yes," and she said, "I'd love a lift in a Rolls-Royce."

'I said, "Oh, OK, where do you live?" She said just around the corner in Shepherd's Bush so I drove her there. She said, "I'd really like to make love to you." I said, "Well,

let's go to my place, then." And we did.'

'The DJs used to get the same treatment as the bands,' agrees Mike Read. 'If I left *TOTP* with Duran Duran, the fans would be like a pack of animals and they'd tear at me as well as them. We were right in the thick of it.

'I remember once Duran flew in by helicopter to avoid the fans and it landed in the BBC car park. I still can't quite believe Health & Safety allowed that one.'

Like a small nation constantly invaded by barbaric armies, Television Centre next had to stand firm against a kamikaze new threat – squadrons of ripped-jean-sporting, peroxide-topped Brosettes.

'We played *TOTP* in 1987 and there were hundreds of screaming lasses at the gates,' says Craig Reid of the Proclaimers. 'We figured they might be there for Bros rather than us.'

By the time Take That fever and Spice Girls mania erupted in the 1990s, *TOTP* production had moved to the relatively inaccessible environs of Elstree, where the fan menace was more easily contained.

Pop worship, however, is a transient creature, and even the most adored teen idols ever to grace *TOTP* would have been wise to take a moment to reflect that, as the late George Harrison once proclaimed, All Things Must Pass.

'*TOTP* invited me back in 2000 to sing "Puppy Love" on a retrospective show,' says Donny Osmond. 'During rehearsals, all these teenage girls were surrounding this little round stage that I was performing on.

'As soon as I started singing, they started screaming. After I had finished the song, I asked them, "Why are you all screaming at me?" And one little girl looked up at me and said, "Because our mums told us to."'

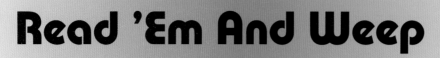

Read 'Em And Weep

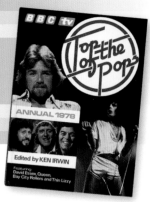

Whenever any brand becomes as iconic as *TOTP* in the 1970s, spin-off merchandising projects invariably follow.

In *TOTP*'s case, this took the form of the *TOTP* annual, published every Christmas by World Distributors from 1974 onwards.

Edited by an anonymous soul named Ken Irwin, these rudimentary tomes combined arch sycophancy towards all music stars with a leaden, local paper-like clichéd prose style that was unlikely to give Nick Kent or Paul Morley any sleepless nights.

The annual came bursting out of the traps in 1974 with a hard-hitting feature titled 'Why The Jacksons Are So Fab!' but really hit its stride the following year.

As transfixed by the show's hosts as by its music stars, Irwin ran 'full-page colour pin-ups' of Jimmy Savile, Tony Blackburn and Noel Edmonds, plus probing interviews with the DJs.

After Edmonds divulged that he had once been an 'Angry Young Man' with 'hairy-fairy' ideas, Dave Lee Travis laid his wacky cards on the table: 'I'm a complete loony. An absolute nutcase. I'll do anything for a laugh.'

Declaring himself 'a really dedicated all-round entertainer' a full three decades before the emergence of David Brent, DLT went on to outline his many talents: 'I'm the Roy Castle of the DJ world … I can sing, dance, tell gags.'

Hints that the feminist revolution had yet to penetrate the world of the *TOTP* annual lay in a feature called 'Adding The Curves To The Pop Scene'.

Lauding Olivia Newton-John as 'a very lively girl, pleasant to look at', Irwin reserved his highest praise for Lynsey de Paul: 'Considered by many menfolk to be the dishiest doll of them all.'

The editor also pandered to his readers' more lascivious needs with a *Jackie*-style heart-throbs spread for which Status Quo, Peters and Lee and Ronnie Laine were arguably rather lucky to make the cut.

With punk setting the musical agenda in 1977, the *TOTP* annual opted for a David Essex front cover, with pin-ups of Gilbert O'Sullivan, Jim Capaldi, Art Garfunkel and Procol Harum.

At a time when the British music press was a cauldron of provocative and audacious analyses of music, Irwin boldly opened 1978's *TOTP* annual with a gushing profile of Demis Roussos.

'He is a mountain of a man, weighing more than 17 stone, with long flowing hair and a thick beard,' the scribe marvelled. 'He looks like an Old Testament prophet.'

It was clearly time to get hip to the beat, daddy-o, and the following year the *TOTP* annual profiled the Jam, Stranglers and

> ## 'Considered by many menfolk to be the dishiest doll of them all.'
>
> **TOTP Annual on Lynsey de Paul**

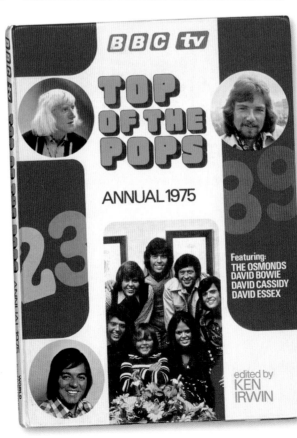

The annuals were an unhappy chapter in *TOTP* history.

Boomtown Rats under the heading 'Punk? It's Revitalised The Rock Scene!'

Thankfully, for non-believers, there was also a wall-friendly, full-page pin-up of John Miles.

The casual sexism raised its head again in 1980 when Mr Irwin's journalistic eye settled on Legs & Co, 'The Girls Who Add Shape To The Show'.

The intrepid editor chatted with Sue Menhenick, 'a vivacious blonde with a stunning 34-24-34 figure' and a woman of trenchant opinions: 'I hate reggae music.'

Nevertheless, DLT would surely have approved of Sue's summary of Legs & Co's mindset: 'There are six

The BBC's guide to popular beat music, 1980.

nutcases here. We are all pretty potty.'

Widening the annual's remit, Irwin also joined Black Sabbath on the road in New York. 'I'm an Englishman,' Ozzy Osbourne told him. 'I don't want to live anywhere else but in England.'

Despite flirting with modernity with cover stars such as Blondie, Adam Ant and Madness, falling sales killed off the *TOTP* annual in 1984. Times had changed, and its staid reportage now looked positively antediluvian next to the flippant approach of the irreverent *Smash Hits* and *Number One*.

As a precursor for what was to happen to *TOTP* 20 years later, it was nigh on perfect.

That Peters and Lee, eh? Phwoargh!

Yule Drive Me Crazy

ever the most serious-minded of programmes, *TOTP* scaled new heights of demented frivolity at Christmas. Straight after the turkey dinner and leading up to the Queen's Speech, Christmas Day *TOTP* was an institution in 20 million British homes.

This was the show that gathered up the year's big hits and No. 1s, wrapped them in bows, ribbons and tinsel, and shoved them out at you in one big glossy, gaudy package.

'Christmas *TOTP* was wonderful,' recalls Dave Lee Travis, fondly. 'The BBC would pull out all the stops and put another £50 in the kitty and we would get sparkly

things, lots of snow and things exploding. It was certainly party time!'

'Those shows had a different feel,' says David Jensen. 'I remember cavalcades of stars, confetti falling like snow, a lot of forced jollity and DJs thrown together and, well, jockeying for position. Pun intended.'

'We would never dream of missing Christmas *TOTP*,' says the Proclaimers' Craig Reid. 'But the TV went off right afterwards, because we were a republican household.'

A perennially upbeat experience, *TOTP* struck a nerve at Christmas, mirroring the national mood of compulsory celebration. Trapped with mind-numbingly tedious aunts,

They do Christmas differently in Wolverhampton.

cousins or grandparents, viewers discerned that John Peel felt just the same about being stuck on a dais with Simon Bates.

Right from *TOTP*'s earliest 1960s days, it was clear that there was something special about the Christmas Day shows, even if things were a tad more genteel back then.

'There was a certain lightness in the air,' remembers Frank Allen of the Searchers. 'It was a great time to gather together and by definition everybody there was a big success. But sadly our fortunes dipped rather severely after 1965, so we didn't get to do very many.'

Given its phenomenal audience figures, there was never any problem attracting artists to Christmas *TOTP*. The 1967 show featured the Rolling Stones, Cliff Richard,

> **'Noel Edmonds and I hosted the 1972 show and for some reason we did it dressed as if we had come out of Sherwood Forest.'**
>
> **Tony Blackburn**

the Bee Gees, Lulu, Procol Harum and a film of the Beatles doing 'All You Need Is Love'.

Unsurprisingly, though, the lewd glam rock 1970s were when Christmas *TOTP* went truly mental and morphed into an orgy of festive fancy dress, Christmas cracker-level quips and unwanted-present sweaters. And that was just the presenters.

'Noel Edmonds and I hosted the 1972 show and for some reason we did it dressed as if we had come out of Sherwood Forest,' reminisces Tony Blackburn. 'We both wore little green hats and jerkins like Robin Hood.

'I gave Pan's People a Christmas present, which was their new girl, Cherry, wrapped in Christmas paper. They unwrapped her and started dancing to Nilsson's

"Without You" in long flowing white dresses.'

The next year, Edmonds and Blackburn's japery involved a running gag where they draped each other in tinsel and baubles like Christmas trees. The nation clutched its aching sides and awaited the show's bawdy climax.

'We were No. 1 at Christmas 1973 with "Merry Christmas Everybody",' says Noddy Holder. "It went in at No. 1 as soon as it was released, two weeks before Christmas, and stayed there for five weeks. God knows who was buying it in the third week of January.

'Two other artists brought out Christmas records

It seemed natural for Tony Blackburn to chortle through 1974's Christmas *TOTP* while his co-host Jimmy Savile, in a Santa outfit, spoke French for no reason whatsoever.

that year, and we stole their thunder. Elton John did "Step Into Christmas" and it only got to No. 24 even though he was huge at the time. Wizzard did "I Wish It Could Be Christmas Every Day" and that got to No. 4.

'We all did the *TOTP* Christmas show and Roy Wood and Wizzard had the hump that they were No. 4 and we were No. 1. So just as we were coming to the end of the song they all ran on stage and splattered me with custard pies.'

In their peerless pomp in 1973, Slade also reprised their No. 1s 'Cum On Feel The Noize' and 'Skweeze Me Pleeze Me' for the same show.

Did anybody order a Christmas pixie?

Mud's Rob Davis (right) had the world's strongest earlobes.

Christmas *TOTP* was such colossal news in those days that it ran in two parts; one on Christmas Day and one on Boxing Day.

'Christmas *TOTP* was bloody hard work because they crammed so much in,' recalls Dave Bartram of Showaddywaddy. 'We could be there for three days. It was fake snow, fake tinsel, fake everything, but they were great to do because everybody watched them.'

Like Christmas Day itself, Yuletide *TOTP* was awaited with a vast sense of anticipation, undercut with the nagging suspicion it could turn out to be a dreary anti-climax.

'It was often a letdown because the records I really liked tended to get to No. 11, not No. 1,' says Johnny Marr. 'I would much rather have seen Mott the Hoople do "All The Young Dudes" than Don McLean singing bloody "Vincent" again.'

Christmas *TOTP*s were never entirely complete without a festive chart-topper: in 1972, Dave Edmunds' 'I Hear You Knocking' hardly seemed adequate. In 1974, Mud topped the heap with the Variety-Club-Elvis croon of 'Lonely This Christmas' and singer Les Gray mimed it as a duet with a Lord Charles-type ventriloquist's dummy.

To Brits, *TOTP*s' myriad eccentricities were the behavioural tics of a well-loved friend. It seemed natural for Tony Blackburn to chortle through

1974's Christmas *TOTP* while his co-host Jimmy Savile, in a Santa outfit, spoke French for no reason whatsoever.

Yet outsiders not versed in *TOTP*'s special-needs behaviour could find its irregular rhythms discomfiting. In 1975, the US country music icon Tammy Wynette enjoyed

Captain Blue and Lord Snooty host Christmas *TOTP*.

an April UK No. 1 with 'Stand By Your Man' then returned in July to play her follow-up, 'D.I.V.O.R.C.E.'

Arriving at the BBC, the jetlagged singer did not seem entirely au fait with, or impressed by, her fellow studio artistes: The Goodies gurning through 'Black Pudding Bertha' and the Wombles playing 'Wombling White Tie and Tails (Foxtrot)'.

Wynette's delicate equilibrium crumbled further when the *TOTP* producers asked her to revisit 'Stand By Your Man' for the Yuletide broadcast and she was suddenly surrounded by not only Christmas trees but also Pan's People, festooned from head to toe in fairy lights.

Shouting 'I thought this was a music programme but it's a goddamn freak show,' a tearful Wynette fled to her dressing room, where her management talked her down. Seventeen years later, she was back on Christmas *TOTP* and happily singing about driving ice cream vans, but that is another story entirely.

If Christmas *TOTP* in the 1970s was ruled by the great clunking fists of big beasts like Savile, Blackburn and DLT, the 1980s brought a new age of democracy as virtually the whole of Radio 1's roster crammed onto the show and old

> ## 'I thought this was a music programme, but it's a goddam freak show.'
>
> **Tammy Wynette,
> TOTP Christmas Special 1975**

faces came out of retirement.

Sharing a mic with the famously vain Noel Edmonds, John Peel's seasonal goodwill to all men was notable by its absence: 'It's a pleasure to be here beside you, Noel. Now I can find out how you get your hair to look like a cake.'

On a return visit to another *TOTP* special, David Hamilton also found the mass onscreen bonhomie did not always survive when the cameras stopped rolling.

'I had to host with Tony Blackburn and Simon Bates, who didn't like each other,' he says. 'They had fallen out and Tony tried to patch things up. He said, "Look, let's forget it and be friends." Simon rejected it and hissed at him, saying, "I don't *want* to be your friend."

'I was standing between them and honestly thought they would come to blows. Then a second later the floor manager cued us in and we were there with our arms round each other like we were the best friends in the world.'

'Yes, well, that falling-out ended up with Simon Bates suing me, so there *was* some bad feeling between us,' sighs Blackburn. 'But it was *TOTP*. We just had to get on with it.'

'The 1980s Christmas *TOTP* were pretty OTT,' admits Janice Long. 'One year we had to dress up as pantomime characters. I was wearing a huge flared skirt, but I had no idea who I was supposed to be.'

'OMD recorded *TOTP* and I watched it on Christmas Day at my parents' house after the turkey dinner,' says Andy McCluskey. 'My mum said, "You look lovely, dear, but why are you all chewing your lips?" I said we were nervous. The truth was we'd just been to the US and discovered cocaine and we were wired off our faces.'

'What's my motivation in this scene, Dave?'

Christmas *TOTP* 1984 saw Band Aid regroup for 'Do They Know It's Christmas' – minus Bono. Insisting that somebody had to mime to every line, the producer Michael Hurll strongarmed a reluctant Paul Weller into mouthing the Irishman's words.

Boy George was in less than festive mood three years later. Scheduled to sing 'Everything I Own' while recovering from heroin addiction, George was angered at not being allowed to serenade the nation in a hat proclaiming 'Fat Pig' and decorated with McDonalds wrappers. He left without performing.

The early 1990s were dark years of Christmas *TOTP* being fronted by people whose own family had hardly heard of them, or, worse, Anthea Turner. Later in the decade, the Yuletide show fell victim to the fad of importing guest presenters.

Take That hosted 1994's Christmas *TOTP*, while the following year saw the odd couple of Jack Dee and the divine Björk. In 1996 the Spice Girls continued their bid for world domination, abetted by Robbie Williams and a rather fortunate Gina G.

In 1999 an original *TOTP* scream idol made a chart-topping return to the Christmas show and was thrown to receive praise from an unexpected quarter.

'Singing "The Millennium Prayer" meant a lot to me because it has a Christian element,' says Cliff Richard. 'A lot of great Christmas hits are just party songs. But while I was on *TOTP* a skinhead in the audience ran up to me, put his thumb up and yelled, "Great record, mate!" I thought, "Oh, goodness me!"'

Christmas Day *TOTP* was not the force it had been. No longer rubbing shoulders with the Queen, it was now reduced to preceding repeat episodes of *Keeping Up Appearances*. Yet it retained the air of distracted, driven jollity that had allowed one band to subvert it nearly 20 years earlier.

'When we did "Up The Junction" on 1979's Christmas *TOTP*, I had always had a hankering to be a singing drummer,' says Squeeze's Glenn Tilbrook. 'So I was. We all swapped instruments and looked totally inappropriate.

'The producers were so busy geeing everybody up that they were blissfully unaware we had even done it.'

Who Do You Do?

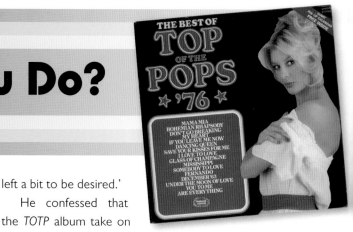

Every single thing about the *TOTP* albums was fake – beginning with the title.

Released by Pickwick Records from 1968 to 1979, these albums of cover versions of chart hits by session musicians had nothing to do with the TV show. The budget label had pulled a quick one after realising that the BBC had neglected to copyright the name.

For 11 years, Pickwick chucked out an album every six weeks, invariably wrapped in a cover of a scantily clad babe (or dolly bird) and recorded in four days or less.

'Your parents would buy them for you and you wouldn't notice it wasn't the real act until you were 11 or 12,' says Clive Jackson of Dr & the Medics. 'By then, you were more interested in the picture of the girl on the cover.'

Pickwick had a crack team of session musicians headed by producer Bruce Baxter and singer Tony Rivers and nobody could accuse them of being less than versatile.

One 1975 album found them covering both Slade's 'In For A Penny' and Laurel and Hardy's 'The Trail Of The Lonesome Pine'. On another, they segued lithely from 'Wombling White Tie And Tails (Foxtrot)' to Kraftwerk's 'Autobahn'.

'There were varying degrees of success,' Baxter admitted to *Mojo* years later. 'Some were very close to the original. Others

> ## 'Some were very close to the original. Others left a bit to be desired.'
>
> **Bruce Baxter, Pickwick producer**

left a bit to be desired.'

He confessed that the *TOTP* album take on Jimi Hendrix's 'Voodoo Chile' 'sounded like Donald Duck'. Tony Rivers reflected that he sang the Sex Pistols' 'Pretty Vacant' 'like Norman Wisdom' and felt Pickwick's take on Donny Osmond's 'Puppy Love' was not a stellar success: 'It was the worst cover version I ever heard.'

Yet at other times, Pickwick were right on the money – even if it was the cover price

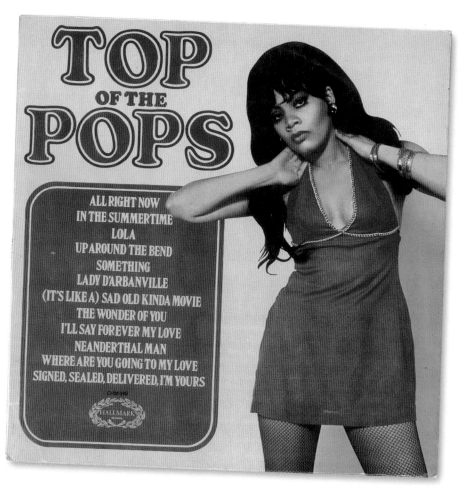

This is what 'sexy stunnas' did before lads' mags were invented.

of 95p in Woolworth.

'Kenny Everett spliced together Queen's "Bohemian Rhapsody" and our version and played them on the radio,' gloated Baxter. 'He said, "I defy anyone to tell me which one they're listening to."'

As a jobbing musician, Elton John sang on early *TOTP* albums, covering Mungo Jerry and Cat Stevens and manually vibrating his throat to produce the Bee Gees' falsetto warble. The ersatz Bryan Ferry, by contrast, was a computer programmer from St Albans.

The critics were not kind. One described the *TOTP* version of Lou Reed's 'Walk On The Wild Side' as 'like a newsreader reading a shopping list' and felt Pickwick's take on Kate Bush's 'Wuthering Heights' evoked Popeye's girl-friend Olive Oyl.

The artists also had decidedly mixed views about these *Stars In Their Eyes* tributes.

'They never knew what the words to our songs were, so they just sang phonetic gibberish,' says Ron Mael of Sparks. 'There again, maybe our words were just gibberish anyway.'

'They couldn't capture our raucousness and never got my singing right,' recalls Noddy Holder, while Nigel Fletcher of Lieutenant Pigeon accuses Pickwick of missing the glory of 'Mouldy Old Dough': 'It hadn't got the magic.'

Dave Cousins was non-plussed by *TOTP*'s mugging of The Strawbs' 'Lay Down': 'There was so much vibrato, it made me sound like a flock of sheep.'

Yet a few musicians fought Pickwick's corner. 'Their versions of our songs were better than ours,' reckons Mike Nolan of Bucks Fizz. 'They were in tune.'

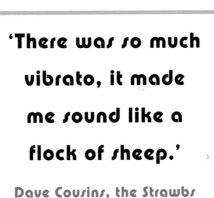

'Wuthering Heights'. 'Ally's Tartan Army'. All human life is here.

'I still have a big collection of *TOTP* albums,' admits Glenn Tilbrook of Squeeze. 'They sang "Cool For Cats" and "Up The Junction". I loved them. They were horrible.'

Pickwick killed off the *TOTP* albums in 1979, when they were haemorrhaging sales to original-hits compilation albums such as *Now That's What I Call Music!* Yet the series – or, rather, its packaging – nearly made a 21st century comeback.

'Status Quo were recording a covers album,' says Francis Rossi. 'We wanted to do the same kind of cover as a joke – a girl with her lunch hanging out, licking a guitar.

'We only didn't do it because we figured, with our luck, people wouldn't get it and would think we were just being lairy rather than funny.'

> '**There was so much vibrato, it made me sound like a flock of sheep.'**
>
> **Dave Cousins, the Strawbs**

Unhinged Melodies

TOTP helped to shift a huge amount of singles. In the format's 1970s and 1980s heyday, major hits regularly sold in excess of one million copies and there was no bigger boost than a spin to 15 million people on Thursday night TV.

TOTP was the first place to see new releases by The Who, Slade, Queen, Madonna, Prince or Michael Jackson. It was also the show that beamed Clive Dunn, Kevin Keegan, Joe Dolce, Tight Fit and Timmy Mallett into the nation's front rooms.

The Top 40 is a broad church that flings open its doors not just to rock, pop and R&B but also to novelty songs, comedy records and crooning soap and sports stars. Democratic to an aesthetic fault, TOTP played the lot.

> ## 'I was amazed by those British novelty acts. The Wombles impressed me in a particular, slightly peculiar way.'
>
> ### Ron Mael, Sparks

'Now, hang on, some novelty records were great!' says Francis Rossi. 'I loved Renée and Renato doing "Save Your Love". It was a great melody, even though the bloke looked like my dad in his worst cardigan.'

Nevertheless, TOTP was notorious for its plummets from the lofty to the laughable, from renowned international artists to tinny cartoon jingles of infinite banality.

Some of the ditties were aimed at children, which means the Wombles, Smurfs, Tweenies, Teletubbies and Mr Blobby can be absolved from a degree of karmic blame. Well, maybe not Mr Blobby.

'I was amazed by those British novelty acts,' Ron Mael, the Sparks keyboardist, recalls. 'The Wombles impressed me in a particular, slightly peculiar way.'

Steeleye Span were less impressed. Having helped out Wombles svengali Mike Batt

No wonder Travolta turned to scientology.

The Wombles: the tidiest band in pop.

by recording 'Super Womble' in secret in 1975, union regulations then required the folk rockers to don the furry costumes and mime it on *TOTP*.

Everybody has a worst *TOTP* moment. Some might plump for Rolf Harris's surreally mawkish 1969 No. 1 'Two Little Boys', or the pith-helmeted Windsor Davies and Don Estelle from *It Ain't Half Hot Mum* gurning through 'Whispering Grass'.

'The worst thing I ever saw on *TOTP* was "The One That I Want" by Hilda Baker and Arthur Mullard,' shudders Tony Blackburn. 'It was horrible.'

Sally Lindsay spent five years as Shelley Unwin in *Coronation Street* and stars in Peter Kay's *Phoenix Nights*, but the actress's closet hides a dark, dark secret.

'I went to St Winifred's School in Stockport,' she says. 'When I was in the infants, the school choir recorded backing vocals for Brian and Michael's "Matchstalk Men and Matchstalk Cats and Dogs". It got to No. 1 in 1978 and they went on *TOTP*.

'When I was seven, I joined the choir and we recorded "There's No One Quite Like Grandma". It got to No. 1 as well so we went down to London on a coach to do *TOTP*. They told us to mime but we didn't know what that meant so we just sang it.

'The teenagers in the audience were staring at us with pure hatred because they had hoped to see something cool such as Duran Duran and they got stuck with us. The director was yelling at them: "Give them a bloody chance! Do a bit of swaying or something!"

Duck soup: Mike Reid.

'We knocked John Lennon's "(Just Like) Starting Over" off No. 1 a week after he was shot dead – how fucking shit is that? We got a £50 book token and we had to pay for our own costumes, but that's the Catholic Church for you, really.'

Novelty records abounded in the 1970s, the decade when naff ruled supreme. 1971 began with *Dad's Army*'s Clive Dunn at No. 1 with the schmaltz-overload 'Grandad' and ended with Benny Hill enjoying a comedic Christmas chart-topper.

'Oh, come on, nobody can criticise "Ernie"!' says Tommy Banner of the Wurzels. 'The words were magic!'

Ray Stevens' 'The Streak' encouraged public nudity while Mike Harding's 'Rochdale Cowboy' and Jasper Carrott smirking through 'Funky Moped' had nobody you knew in stitches during their *TOTP* airings.

The short-lived CB radio fad propelled the US singer CW McCall to No. 2 with the 1976 truckers' anthem 'Convoy' but this didn't prepare Britain for the horror of what was to follow.

'I decided to do a spoof so my Radio 1 colleague Paul Burnett and I became Laurie Lingo and the Dipsticks and recorded "Convoy GB",' chuckles Dave Lee Travis. 'It got to No. 4 – and was No. 1 in Luxembourg!

'We did it on *TOTP* as our characters, Super Scouse and Plastic Chicken. Paul was in a chicken outfit and I sat on the floor in a white superhero costume with a steering wheel in front of me. It was outrageous, but so much fun.'

The Goodies capered though the 1970s with a string of humour-bypass hits, including 'Black Pudding Bertha' and 'Funky Gibbon'. After playing the latter on *TOTP*, they sang impromptu backing vocals on that week's No. 1, David Essex's 'Gonna Make You A Star'.

The decade also saw future *EastEnders* actor Mike Reid administer a Cockney rhyming slang kicking to 'The Ugly Duckling' and *Kojak* star Telly Savalas visit *TOTP* to drawl through the sentimental hokum of his spoken-word No. 1, 'If'.

All this paled into insignificance, however, next to 'Mouldy Old Dough'.

'I was in the BBC bar with Slade when Lieutenant Pigeon came to *TOTP*,' says Francis Rossi. 'This geezer came in with what looked like his nan, and Noddy said, "What the fuck are things coming to?"'

'Mouldy Old Dough' was a lop-sided lurch of ragtime boogie-woogie recorded in a semi-detached in Coventry by Nigel Fletcher, Rob Woodward and Rob's 58-year-old mother Hilda, whose bingo wings flapped as she smilingly attacked an old Joanna on *TOTP*. It was No. 1 for four weeks.

'Rob and I were in a band called Staveley Makepiece, who had already been on *TOTP*,' says Fletcher. 'We did "Mouldy Old Dough" as Lieutenant Pigeon as a novelty sideline. Rob thought of the title and told me to sing it in a growling voice. I asked him what it meant and he said he had no idea.

'It was too oddball for everybody, then a Belgian TV current affairs show started using it as their theme tune and somehow it became a hit. We were as surprised as anybody.'

'It was, beyond a doubt,' says Graham Gouldman of 10cc solemnly, 'the most singular and bizarre thing that I ever heard on *TOTP*.'

Lieutenant Pigeon's near-identical follow-up, 'Desperate Dan', was a lesser success and they returned to the anonymity that spawned them. Some bands, however, made a career out of comedy records.

The Barron Knights and the

Telly Savalas replaces a lollipop with a microphone.

It ain't half grot, Mum: Don Estelle and Windsor Davies.

Wurzels made spasmodic *TOTP* appearances through the 1970s, the latter scoring a 1976 No. 1 with 'The Combine Harvester (Brand New Key)'. The 1980s, though, belonged to Black Lace.

The comic duo of Colin Gibb and the late Alan Barton specialised in corny songs that hit big in the clubs of Benidorm and holidaymakers then bought on their return home. They often came with a dance routine attached.

'We would always try to make the *TOTP* studio audience join in,' says Gibb. 'It wasn't hard – there were only about 30 of them.'

Gibb is stoical about Black Lace's status in musical history: '"Agadoo" got voted the second-worst single ever and we asked for a recount because we thought it should be first.' Yet he was still sometimes hurt by *TOTP*'s endemic snobbery.

'Peter Powell used to do the album chart rundown on his Radio 1 show,' he recalls. 'He never played anything off our album, even if we were Top 5, because he wanted to be hip.'

'He had to introduce us on *TOTP*, and at the end he came running over and said, "Guys, I'm so sorry I never play you on the radio, but it would ruin my show."'

'Another time, we were standing next to Howard Jones by the side of a stage. I said, "Hiya, how are you doing?" and he put his nose in the air and walked off.'

This was harsh of Jones, whose own 'New Song', complete with a mime artist in chains illustrating the line '*Throw off your mental chains*' with Pan's People-like literalness, was one of the most unintentionally hilarious moments in *TOTP* history.

Cliff Richard has never viewed himself as a novelty artist, but

ventured into comedy in 1986 with the stars of *The Young Ones* when they rerecorded his 1959 hit 'Living Doll'.

'I wasn't a great fan of the show because I thought some of the humour was horrific,' he admits. 'But I used to watch it because I knew they mentioned me every now and then.

'When they asked me to do the record, I said, "Hey, guys, I've spent 30 years building an image that people respect and is good for Britain, and I could blow it in this one song."

'They promised to be respectful, cleaned up their act and we sold a lot of records for charity. They whacked me on the head with a mallet but that was fine. I tried to look cool in the photos, like we rock stars do, but, gosh, they all had their fingers up their noses!'

Novelty records could breed their own irony. Isaac Hayes is one of the towering figures of 1970s US funk, but his sole *TOTP* No. 1 came in cartoon form as *South Park*'s Chef singing 'Chocolate Salty Balls' in 1998.

Before he visited *TOTP* with Bassomatic and then reinvented Madonna's career, dance producer William

> ## '"Agadoo" got voted the second-worst single ever and we asked for a recount because we thought it should be first.'
>
> ### Colin Gibb, Black Lace

Lieutenant Pigeon: not quite the Beatles.

Orbit wrote 'Loadsamoney' for Harry Enfield and appeared on the show with him. 'I was dressed as a plumber, waving a saw,' he recalls.

In 1991, *Monty Python's Flying Circus* made No. 3 with 'Always Look On The Bright Side Of Life' and Eric Idle paraded around the studio as it collapsed around him. This doubtless amused the kind of people who can recite the Dead Parrot Sketch in its entirety.

Football and *TOTP* were rarely happy bedfellows, from Hoddle and Waddle's white-suited 1987 turn with 'Diamond Lights' to Gazza bellowing 'Fog On The Tyne' like a man who had learned both singing and English via correspondence course.

The Wurzels. Banjo. Souzaphone. Accordion. The classic rock 'n' roll line-up.

Chas & Dave accompanied the Tottenham Hotspur FA Cup Final Squad to the show in 1981 to play 'Ossie's Dream' and made a return trip the following year for 'Tottenham Tottenham'. Six years later, Billy Bragg met the England football team at *TOTP*.

'They were miming and clapping along,' he remembers. 'The only person who couldn't clap in time was Peter Shilton, the goalkeeper. That was quite disturbing.'

They were never cool and nor would they make a DVD of *TOTP*'s finest moments, but novelty records made their creators' names – and they remained loyal to them.

'I don't care if people think "Combine Harvester" was the worst No. 1 ever,' says Tommy Banner of the Wurzels. 'I just wish somebody would write another one as bad for us.'

Spurs return to the scene of the crime.

Nul Points For Style

The Eurovision Song Contest and *TOTP* are obvious kindred spirits. One is a glorious bonfire of the inanities, a gaudy and hyperactive celebration of all that is daft, tacky and addictive about pop music.

The other is the Eurovision Song Contest.

Jingoistic to a fault, *TOTP* invariably cheered Britain's Eurovision entry off to the contest with the fervour of a dockside crowd waving Our Brave Boys off to war, rather than to trill an inane ditty in Rotterdam.

'We did *TOTP* the week before Eurovision,' remembers Cheryl Baker of Bucks Fizz, who won the contest in 1981 with 'Making Your Mind Up'.

'The *TOTP* producers gave everybody in the studio balloons and Union Jacks. It was like the last night of the Proms.'

Winning British entrants

were similarly welcomed back to *TOTP* like returning heroes, as Brotherhood of Man found out after 'Save Your Kisses For Me' triumphed in The Hague in 1976.

'We ended up being No. 1 for six weeks and it was such a celebration at *TOTP* that all the audience were doing the dance with us off camera,' recalls Nicky Stevens.

'Some of them were pretty good at it. Some of them… well, they all did their best.'

Lynsey de Paul sat back-to-back at grand pianos with Mike Moran for 1977 entry 'Rock Bottom', while two years later Black Lace were a four-piece and not yet comedy artistes when they represented Britain in Jerusalem with 'Mary Ann'.

'We were doing cabaret in Wales when we won A Song For Europe, so this little venue that had booked an ordinary band suddenly had overnight stars,' says Black Lace's Colin Gibb.

> '**It was such a celebration at TOTP that all the audience were doing the dance with us off camera.'**
>
> **Nicky Stevens, Brotherhood of Man**

Brotherhood of Man's aerobics video was not a success.

'They wouldn't release us from our contract so our record label hired us a Winnebago to race to *TOTP* and then back to Wales again to do the cabaret.'

High-profile entry Sandie Shaw was Britain's first Eurovision winner in 1967 with 'Puppet On A String', a bizarre outcome after she dismissed it as a 'stupid cuckoo clock tune'.

However, a patriotic Cliff Richard failed to repeat her success with 'Congratulations' the following year and 'Power To All Our Friends' in 1973.

'I went on *TOTP* with both songs and the audiences were just so encouraging,' Cliff remembers fondly now.

'People ask me why I did Eurovision and I tell them, "Hey! It gave me the chance to sing my song to 400 million people and a million of them bought it, thank you very much!"'

Occasionally, *TOTP* was forced to acknowledge that other countries entered Eurovision and reluctantly opened its doors to Europop.

After triumphing in glamorous Harrogate in 1982, 18-year-old German chanteuse Nicole

'Is his bigger than mine?' Lynsey de Paul gets pianist's envy.

serenaded the show with the Lisa Simpson-pop of 'A Little Peace', while Abba became *TOTP* stalwarts after 'Waterloo' blasted them to fame in 1974.

Yet Katrina & the Waves' easy 1997 victory with 'Love Shine A Light' was not the making of the band, but the undoing – and they proceeded to unravel on *TOTP*.

'Our guitarist, Kimberley Rew, thought Eurovision was so uncool that he refused to play in the contest in Dublin,' explains Katrina Leskanich.

'After we won, he deigned to share our glory on *TOTP*. We played the show three more times and each time the spirit in the band had got worse.

'By our last performance we were sitting at separate tables in the canteen, getting drunk and having stand-up rows in the dressing room.

'Then we were stumbling on stage to mime "Love Shine A Light". I guess you can say it was fairly ironic.'

Bucks Fizz: a simple song required primary colours.

I'm So Bored Of *TOTP*

Not everybody fell for *TOTP*'s idiosyncratic charms. Over the years, a handful of artists declined all invitations to appear on the show, for reasons ranging from strongly held principle to terminal muddle-headedness.

Led Zeppelin were the first high-profile refuseniks, although as they never actually did anything as bourgeois as release a single, their stance was fairly irrelevant. It was also highly ironic: from 1968 to 1981 and 1998 to 2003, CCS's souped-up version of Zeppelin's 'Whole Lotta Love' served as *TOTP*'s theme tune.

In *TOTP*'s final years, Arctic Monkeys passed on all invites to the show, even when they were at No. 1. However, as they also pass on attending the Brits and everything else apart from making pimply, truculent singles about being dumped, it probably wasn't personal.

Yet by far the most famous and long-running boycott

> **'It was stupid – not playing TOTP had absolutely no chance of changing anything in the world.'**
>
> **Jet Black, the Stranglers**

of *TOTP* was by The Clash. Right from their debut single 'White Riot' in April 1977, the punk icons' pursuit of authenticity led them to declare White City a no-go zone as they objected to *TOTP*'s 'phoney' practice of requiring bands to mime.

The Clash's principles were often confused – they condemned stadium rock before playing New York's 60,000-capacity Shea Stadium – but at least they had some. Yet their high-minded disdain for *TOTP* disappointed more acolytes than it delighted.

'I was always really upset when they wouldn't do *TOTP*,' says Inspiral Carpets' Clint Boon. 'It was the only way a kid in Oldham like me could get to see them.'

'I used to call it The Clash Conundrum,' says Nick Tesco of punk/new wave band the Members, who appeared on *TOTP* in 1979 with 'Sound of the Suburbs'. 'Were they really being subversive or was Ian Dury being more subversive in

Led Zeppelin, not on *TOTP*.

The Clash never made the short trip from the Westway to Shepherd's Bush.

going on *TOTP* and singing a song like "Hit Me With Your Rhythm Stick"?

'The Clash could afford not to play *TOTP*. It was ironic because they were signed to CBS, a huge American multi-media corporation, and most of the punk bands like us were signed to independents – but we were the ones who were seen as selling out!'

The ironies multiplied in 1980, when The Clash's usual *TOTP* veto resulted in Legs & Co dancing to 'Bankrobber' complete with cartoon face masks and swag bags, and again in 1991, when a Levi's ad propelled 'Should I Stay Or Should I Go?' to No. 1. The producers showed a video.

'The Clash not playing *TOTP* used to piss me off,' says Billy Bragg. 'You have to get your ideas across by any means necessary and that is not achieved by having bloody Legs & Co prance around to your song.'

Joe Strummer finally appeared

on *TOTP* before his death when he supplied a guest vocal on Black Grape's 1996 football single, 'England's Irie'. Perhaps it was a tacit admission of regret for a policy that, while noble, appeared misguided even to his punk compadres.

'It was stupid – not playing *TOTP* had absolutely no chance of changing anything in the world,' concludes Jet Black of the Stranglers, while the Damned's Rat Scabies is equally dismissive of The Clash's ideo-logical stance.

'The whole point of making records is for people to hear them,' he argues. 'Why make a single, then not play it on the BBC programme that plays singles?

'Ultimately, what The Clash did was elitist – it was the kind of thing that King Crimson or Yes might do. I'm afraid it was them either trying to be cool or being very naïve.'

The Arctic Monkeys staged a puzzling, nay, pointless boycott.

Subvert And Destroy

Punk rock was angry. *TOTP* was pathologically cheery. Punk was rooted in protest. *TOTP* was apolitical. Punk was predicated on authenticity. *TOTP* was mimed and schmaltzy. Punk was anti-Establishment. *TOTP* was filmed at the heart of the BBC.

It was never going to be an easy relationship.

Punk's two prime movers hardly figured on *TOTP*. The Clash banned themselves, and after the furore surrounding 'Anarchy In The UK' and 'God Save The Queen', the Sex Pistols were only seen on video. Yet this didn't lessen the BBC's twitchiness towards the new wave.

'*TOTP* were so wary of us,' says The Damned's Rat Scabies. 'They'd get us in and out of the building as quickly as possible. Until they realised we didn't bite, they wouldn't

> ## 'Until they realised we didn't bite, they wouldn't even let us in the BBC canteen.'
>
> **Rat Scabies, The Damned**

even let us in the BBC canteen.'

'The BBC were paranoid about what we might do,' concurs Jet Black of the Stranglers. 'They clearly believed everything they had read in the tabloids.

'Before our first appearance, the *NME* had written, "The Stranglers are going on *TOTP* tomorrow, they're bound to smash the place up!" So when we got there, we asked for brushes and dusters and spent the day cleaning the dressing room.'

Siouxsie and the Banshees, the Buzzcocks, the Ruts, Billy Idol, Sham 69 and even the Exploited all beat a path to Television Centre, yet these shock troops of the new order found pop's Home Guard still defiantly *in situ*.

'There was a crossover period where we'd be there with the Buzzcocks but also Racey and Showaddywaddy,'

The Buzzcocks were punky *TOTP* regulars.

remembers Glenn Tilbrook of Squeeze. 'That weird formula pop music was still going strong.'

'Actually, a lot of the punk bands seemed scared of us,' notes Dave Bartram of Showaddywaddy. 'We were big blokes, there were a lot of us, and they thought we were real Teds.'

'I remember introducing the Rich Kids, which was Midge Ure, Glen Matlock and Rusty Egan,' says David Jensen. 'Then when they had finished, we segued straight into Terry Wogan singing "The Floral Dance".'

'We always seemed to be on at the same time as The Jam,' recalls Nicky Stevens of Brotherhood of Man. 'Paul Weller was a very nice, polite young man.'

If *TOTP* was nervous of punk's rebel rockers, they also arrived with their own mental baggage. Rat Scabies had never trusted the show since he first set eyes on it.

'It was always a programme about the Establishment and the artists that were accepted by the Establishment,' he says. 'Because it was the BBC, it was notoriously non-revolutionary.

'It always seemed to be full of insipid pop tunes and the presenters were like your dad or your uncle. They used to make me think of Ford Cortinas and Harry Fenton's clothes.

'Yet the first time we went on, I didn't know how to handle it. I thought, "My God, this is *Top of the fucking Pops*, what am I going to do?" I started taking the piss by miming really badly and the camera just swung off me straight away.'

Sham 69's Jimmy Pursey: 'Have Showaddywaddy gone yet?'

> ## 'Paul Weller was a very nice, polite young man.'
>
> **Nicky Stevens, Brotherhood of Man**

'On our first appearance I was excited despite myself, but it was a massive anti-climax,' recalls Nick Tesco of the Members. 'There was a sense of unreality – we were doing the biggest thing in our career to date and it seemed bollocks.

'We played a gig at the Hope & Anchor that night and that left more of an impression on me.'

For kids in the provinces, glimpsing a slash of punk militancy on *TOTP* could be a life-changing experience. 'You'd see the Buzzcocks or the Stranglers and they would stick out a mile,' says

The Jam: went home via the tube station, at midnight.

Clint Boon. 'It showed how bland other things were.

'When I was 17 I saw the Adverts on *TOTP* and I was that excited that I managed to get all the way from Oldham to a little club on the moors outside Preston to see them play that same night. It was genuinely inspiring.'

Nevertheless, punk's radical musical revolution failed to co-opt some of *TOTP*'s more old-school presenters. 'I hated punk rock,' confesses Tony Blackburn. 'It left me cold. I didn't like one thing about it.'

In his case, the sentiment was mutual. When Elvis Costello played 'Radio Radio' on *TOTP* in 1978, he pointed at Blackburn as he sang '*The radio is in the hands of such a lot of fools*.' Blackburn grinned back, impervious to what was going on.

'The DJs were horrible,' sighs Nick Tesco. 'Even when they were young, they were old. They represented that whole world before punk where popular music had to be talked down to the youth.

'You'd be in the BBC bar, off your head on speed, and that twat DLT would be in there, smoking his pipe and recounting to his chums the wacky time he drank six pints of bitter with Smokie. I would think, "You just so don't get it, do you?"'

Jimmy Savile, of course, had seen them come and seen them go. Having survived the Rolling Stones and Alice Cooper, he wasn't about to be afraid of the Skids.

'One punk rock band came in,' he recalls. 'They were pussycats all day, then when they finished, one of them had half a cup of tea in a paper cup. He suddenly remembered that he was supposed to be a punk so he threw the tea.

'Everybody went, "Ooh!" and he said, "Sorry!"'

By contrast, nothing threw Savile, as was exemplified when he used a screening of the video for the Sex Pistols' 'C'mon Everybody' as the cue for an impromptu road safety lecture.

> ## 'I hated punk rock. It left me cold. I didn't like one thing about it.'
>
> **Tony Blackburn**

The Stranglers' Hugh Cornwell, shortly after the band's Mr Sheen frenzy.

'Now then, guys and gals, you will notice Sidney Vicious is not wearing a crash helmet on his motorbike!' stressed the *Jim'll Fix It* host. 'You must never, never do that!'

Ultimately, Britain's State-sponsored pop show and punk's insurrectionists arrived at a strategic truce. *TOTP* gained valuable credibility by association; the bands shifted a lot more records. There was something in it for both parties.

'Once people on *TOTP* realised we weren't going to spit at them, they were fine,' concedes Tesco. Even the Sex Pistols were eventually to go on *TOTP*, playing two songs when they re-formed in middle age

for 1996's *Filthy Lucre* tour.

TOTP was a conveyor belt and the punks took their place on it. Finding it impossible to smash the system, they satisfied themselves with minor guerrilla raids.

'Peter Powell was doing an introduction, and Jools [Holland] and I ran behind him and pogoed up and down with our fingers up each other's noses,' says Glenn Tilbrook. 'They had no time to retake it so it went out. We got red carded from the BBC bar.'

'I used to black out one of my teeth to look anti-*TOTP*,' boasts Rat Scabies. 'It was a little victory.'

'When we mimed, I'd ignore the mic and walk around singing the wrong words,' says Nick Tesco. 'But I'd never do anything too bad, in case they didn't let us on there again.'

> ## 'Once people on TOTP realised we weren't going to spit at them, they were fine.'
>
> **Nick Tesco, the Members**

The Damned: Mr Scabies' subversive blacked-out tooth not pictured.

BANDS
WON'T PLAY
NO MORE
TOO MUCH
FIGHTING
ON THE
DANCE FLOOR

Ooh, Bit Of Politics!

Exuberant, glossy and gloriously superficial, *TOTP* cleaved joyously to the poptastic view that the medium was the message. This unwavering cheeriness could prove discomfiting for visiting artists who felt that the message was, well, the message.

It was a brave performer indeed who ventured on to *TOTP*'s weekly sugar rush with Something To Say and did so while surrounded by gaudy lights, perma-grinning DJs and a blithely partying audience. But some of them tried.

'Elvis Costello was on *TOTP* singing "Shipbuilding", a very desolate protest song against the Falklands War,' Martyn Ware of Heaven 17 once marvelled. 'He was in the middle of exotic dancers in cages and the whole audience were whooping.'

The Specials fared little better in 1981. David Jacobs had been exhumed for the show's 900th edition and was roundly perplexed by 'Ghost Town', the Two-Tone band's hard-hitting account of the economic effect of Thatcherism

on Britain's industrial heartlands: 'Oh dear, that wasn't very cheery, was it?'

'It did feel weird playing a song like "Sound of the Suburbs" on a pop show like *TOTP*,' admits Nick Tesco of the Members. 'But that's all there was. They weren't going to let us on *Multi-Coloured Swap Shop*. *TOTP* was our only outlet.'

The BBC's charter meant few bands got the chance to mount a soapbox and perform hard-edged political material on *TOTP*. Yet when the folk-pop group The Strawbs got a rare opportunity in 1971, they scored a spectacular own goal.

'*TOTP* let us play an album track and we chose "The Hangman and the Papist", a deadly serious song about the sectarian divide in Northern Ireland,' recalls singer Dave Cousins.

'I started singing, glanced around and saw our

Far from cheery: the non-poptastic Specials.

The Members address the nation's youth.

keyboardist, Rick Wakeman, grinning away and playing his organ with a paint roller. I could have killed him.

'Then when we played "Part of the Union", our trade union song, Viv Stanshall from the Bonzo Dog Doo Dah band happened to be there and came looming up from behind our piano with a candelabrum on his head.'

A newcomer at the pop/politics interface, Billy Bragg was surprised but impressed when a *TOTP* presenter appeared willing to go the extra mile when he appeared in 1985 singing 'Between The Wars', his paean to socialism and union rights.

'Steve Wright was hosting the show, and he came over at rehearsal and asked me to explain the politics of the song to help him with his intro,' he says. 'I talked him through it and he listened thoughtfully and nodded a lot. Then when it came to the show, he just said, "Ladies and gentlemen, it's Billy Bragg!"

> ## 'The show was full of bands like Wham! shoving shuttlecocks down their shorts. I felt like a fish out of water.'
>
> **Billy Bragg**

'The show was full of bands like Wham! shoving shuttlecocks down their shorts. I felt like a fish out of water. The director told all the audience to wave their hands in the air, so I went over and told him, "Look, mate, it's not really very appropriate."'

Yet in the show's dog days, Bragg made a final trip to *TOTP* in a valiant bid to convince the nation's youth of the merits of republicanism.

'I got to sing "Take Down The Union Jack", my protest song against the Queen's golden jubilee, on the night before the jubilee in 2002,' he explains.

'*TOTP* stuck me on a table that was dressed up for a street party. They stood me among the jellies and trifles and cakes, bleeped out some of the words, and all these kids just stared up at me, thinking, "What the *fuck* is this old geezer doing?"'

Billy Bragg: this guitar kills fascists.

This Is The New Pop

Pop goes in cycles and *TOTP*, when it was on form, spun the wheels adroitly. As the 1980s dawned, the show underwent a make-over that mirrored the shiny, glossy music that it was now beginning to showcase.

After the austerity of punk and new wave, the New Romantics embraced dressing-up, self-celebration and larger-than-life pop with big ideas. *TOTP* reacted by turning itself into a frenetic nightclub, accentuating the positive and going back to the future.

'Duran, Spandau and us saw it as a continuation of the glam *TOTP* we had grown up with,' Martyn Ware of Heaven 17 reflected. 'We donned Antony Price suits, but it was a time when even 40-year-old singers suddenly came on in eyeliner.'

I had never wanted to be a musician, I wanted to be a pop star,' admitted Duran Duran's John Taylor, with engaging honesty. 'I just wanted to go on TOTP, not up and down in the back of a transit van for 10 years.'

It has become a habit to dismiss early 1980s synth-pop as an era of superficial decadence, a triumph of style over substance, but in truth a generation of bands used *TOTP* to pursue an ideal of intelligent, visceral, perfect pop.

The Human League's Phil Oakey sought to roll the world into a question from beneath a radically lop-sided haircut. ABC, Spandau Ballet and Duran Duran looked to revolt into style. Simple Minds chased their New Gold Dream. All felt

> ## 'We wanted Spandau Ballet to be new and not look like anybody had ever looked on TOTP before.'
>
> **Gary Kemp**

Spandau Ballet: one day, nobody will dress like this.

they represented a clean break from the past.

'Absolutely!' says Andy McCluskey of OMD. 'We thought we were the future. Guitar bands were stereotypes, monolithic, the Anti-Christ – get out of our way!'

'We went on *TOTP* with Cliff Richard, Elton John and Bonnie Tyler and I thought, "Christ Almighty, what is this shite?" We *knew* we were taking over.'

'We totally felt we were sweeping away the old guard,' agrees Gary Kemp. 'We wanted Spandau to be new and not look like anybody had ever looked on *TOTP* before.'

Nevertheless, Spandau found there was one practical downside to a social milieu formed exclusively of arts students, designers and poseurs.

'We didn't have any roadies when we started because the only people that we knew were fashionistas with no ambition ever to pick up an amp in their lives,' Kemp recalls.

Duran Duran. It's all about the music, right?

'One friend designed our lighting in a Bauhaus impressionistic style and came with us to our first *TOTP* in his best black Seditionaries gear, but he refused to get out of the van to do any shifting, so we had to set up all our stage gear ourselves.'

For its part, *TOTP* happily became a weekly Club Tropicana. Zoot suits, vertiginous hair and cheerleaders planted in the audience were in, as was a presentational style as zingy and upbeat as the music it introduced.

'It was the 1980s, so if it was a bow, it was big!' Janice Long remembered. 'If it was a colour, it was the most vibrant! My outfits normally cost more than my fee.

'I remember people going round trying to get everybody to dance, everybody banging into each other, huge hair styles, padded shoulders and dancers who looked like wood stain. It was funny standing there while it was

> 'It was the 1980s, so if it was a bow, it was big! If it was a colour, it was the most vibrant!'
>
> **Janice Long**

going on – but it worked on the telly.'

The Associates gave an unforgettable display of demented narcissism. Adam Ant had a dance troupe on each of the three stages for 'Goody Two Shoes'.

One of the original New Romantic pioneers, though, found it hard to affect the languid cool that was the era's emotional default setting.

'Every time I did *TOTP*, I'd get there as early as they would let me in and spend the day hanging out trying to look at famous people,' admits Gary Numan. 'Even when I was No. 1, I never really felt like a pop star myself.

Gary Numan gazes in awe at Toto Coelo.

'It was always fascinating and I was just so happy to be there. I'd go around the studio saying hello to the camera crew, the woman selling the drinks, everybody.'

From his No. 1 debut single 'Are Friends Electric?' on, Numan became known for his sub-Thin White Duke, pallid visage, yet this alien aspect resulted from a happy accident in the *TOTP* make-up room.

'The first time I turned up, I had spots, so the make-up ladies gave me very pale-looking make-up to cover them,' he divulges. 'The whole white face thing became very

Basildon's Depeche Mode: so modern, they even came from a new town.

powerful, so I kept the image.'

Glenn Gregory of Heaven 17 was less lucky with his visits to *TOTP*'s resident slaphappy cosmetics division.

'I could never work out why you had to go to the make-up room for these women to cover you in orange make-up with a big fat sponge,' he complains.

'They just had this big tub of orange and liberally whacked it all over your face. You looked like you'd been guzzling carotene for your entire life.'

'The make-up room was definitely the place to go for *TOTP* gossip,' remembers Clive Jackson, singer of Dr & the Medics. 'They were very indiscreet and would happily tell you who was going bald or receding.'

TOTP's mascara-sporting new synth-pop warriors may have been united in their wish to sweep away the rockist old guard but they presented a far from united front. These were individualist times and sartorial rivalries were matters of life and death.

'The competition between acts in the 1980s was so intense,' Gary Kemp admits. 'What we wore on *TOTP* was so important.

'Everybody was hunkered down in their dressing room, saying, "Oh my God, somebody else has got on the same Gaultier that I wanted to wear! Quick, run out and get me something else!"'

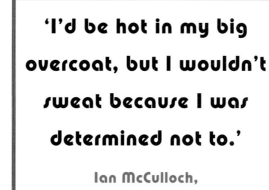

'I'd be hot in my big overcoat, but I wouldn't sweat because I was determined not to.'

Ian McCulloch,
Echo & the Bunnymen

'The only time there was any kind of party backstage was when Duran Duran were on,' says Johnny Marr. 'They would normally come in still up and at it from the night before.'

'In the 1980s a new bitchiness came into pop thanks to things like *Smash Hits*, who encouraged bands to slag each other off,' remembers Soft Cell's Marc Almond. 'Then you'd bump into them at *TOTP*.

'Spandau and Duran would arrive with a great flurry and huge entourages and have these choice dressing rooms, and we would be the poor Northerners, shoved into a cupboard somewhere.'

Depeche Mode played tinny, chirpy ditties unrecognisable from their portentous electro-goth of today. Wham! sang about loving life on the dole. Japan dreamed up a still music that seemed to hover on the verge of silence.

'My big thing was projecting untouchability,' reflects Echo and the Bunnymen singer, Ian McCulloch. 'I'd be hot in my big overcoat under the studio lights but I wouldn't sweat because I was determined not to.'

When idealists are striving to create a brave new world, they resent remnants of the past. Some synth-poppers were comfortable with Mike Read, David Jensen and Janice Long, who championed their music on Radio 1, but felt contempt for *TOTP*'s old guard.

'The first time Duran Duran were on *TOTP*, I told Simon le Bon he looked like a young Elvis Presley,' says Mike Read. 'He looked bewildered.'

'I would have bands like The Police or The Pretenders in session on my radio show, then later they would turn up on *TOTP*,' says David Jensen. 'It was an exciting time.'

'We hated it when we had

Pop revolutionaries OMD wished death on all *TOTP* presenters over 30.

Kylie: the acceptable face of Stock Aitken Waterman.

to us, mouthing the words and ripping up pieces of coloured paper,' bassist David McClymont later told journalist Simon Goddard.

'We were furious but were told we had no choice so I went to the bar and got drunk out of my mind. I remember going to make-up and telling them I wanted my eyes to be as black as possible, like in old silent movies.

'When we played, they had to cut between cameras quickly because I fell off the stage. The next week our label, Polydor, told us we had been banned by *TOTP*.'

Lesser lights such as Visage, Fiction Factory, Flock of Seagulls and Classix Nouveaux emerged in the slipstream of the New Romantic pioneers, but by 1984 the brash Frankie Goes To Hollywood ruled the *TOTP* roost.

Possibly seeking to exact revenge for the banning of the lairy 'Relax', Holly Johnson hit on a way to get a little extra for his licence fee.

'You could get your whole week's ironing done at *TOTP*,' he claimed.

to endure the dinosaur DJs introducing us,' admits OMD's McCluskey. 'I'd think, "Jimmy Savile, Dave Lee Travis, you sad old fuckers – don't you think it's time you gave up?"'

Yet *TOTP* remained set in its ways and it would take a gale-force wind of change to blow away its most enduring peccadilloes, as Scottish guitar band Orange Juice found when they had a head-on collision with the ever-literal creative vision of Zoo choreographer Flick Colby.

'We were doing "Rip It Up" on a live *TOTP* and the producers told us that Legs & Co would be dancing next

'You just took all your clothes in and asked them, "Oh, I don't know what to wear – can you iron all these things so I can decide, please?"'

Pet Shop Boys and New Order emerged to carry the torch for quixotic, questing electro-pop but by the mid-1980s the fantastical New Gold Dream was fading fast.

By 1986, overwrought, over-emoting coffee-table soul ruled the *TOTP* roost, with every show seemingly featuring some dead-eyed combination of Phil Collins, Simply Red, Lisa Stansfield, Sade, The Style Council and Simon Bates ogling Tina Turner's legs.

The nation also developed an inexplicable taste for Pete Waterman's fluffy conveyor-belt pop, with Stock Aitken Waterman's roster of Rick Astley, Sonia, Big Fun, Page 3 girl Sam Fox and two *Neighbours* stars, Kylie Minogue and Jason Donovan, suddenly ubiquitous.

Kylie and Jason even scored a 1988 Christmas No. 1 with 'Especially For You', despite dashing straight from Heathrow Airport to a live *TOTP* to improvise their way through a dance routine they'd had no chance to rehearse.

Nevertheless, for most *TOTP* fans, the 1980s will forever be the decade of rouge, kohl, eyeliner and preposterously

> ## 'You could get your whole week's ironing done at *TOTP*.'
>
> **Holly Johnson**

ambitious and boundaries-pushing pop music, even if the look favoured by its makers has not aged as well as it might.

'Shortly after the BBC started showing *TOTP2*, they featured one of our early 1980s appearances, when I was all in make-up with my mad hair,' says Eddie Lundon, guitarist with China Crisis.

'My son was watching. It slowly dawned on him that it was his dad and he kept looking at me, then back at the TV, then back at me, with his mouth hanging open. Then he said: "Oh my God! Oh no!"

'He looked so ashamed. How old was he? Five.'

The Pet Shop Boys' rider included a couple of ginger nuts.

Dude looks like A lady

It began, as so many things did, with David Bowie. When a lavishly made-up Ziggy Stardust draped an arm round Spider from Mars Mick Ronson during 'Starman' in July 1972, *TOTP* witnessed its first provocatively androgynous pop star.

It was not to be its last.

Glam heaved with pouting boys who looked like girls who looked like boys who looked like girls. Despite the fact that the rest of his band resembled a moonlighting gang of plasterers, Mud guitarist Rob Davis special-ised in skin-tight leopard-skin catsuits and earrings he was in danger of tripping over.

The preferred *TOTP* look *du jour* of Sweet's guitarist Steve Priest was liberally applied lipstick and smudged mascara beneath his German stormtrooper helmet. Like most of the post-Bolan/Bowie glam icons, he looked both comically camp and resolutely heterosexual.

By contrast Roxy Music's Brian Eno, splendid in velvet bodices and peacock feathers, looked less like a trannie than an asexual space alien with identity issues. Heaven 17's Martyn Ware described Eno as a 'glam Max Wall', which was slightly unfair (but only slightly).

Punk had little truck with androgyny, but gender bending returned to *TOTP* with the dawn of the New Romantic era. The Smiths' debut appearance in November 1983 came directly after the

> ## 'It did look like I had a bag of onions down my crotch. But that's Vivienne Westwood for you.'
>
> **Pete Burns**

magnificently spangly glamour puss Marilyn singing 'Calling Your Name'.

'He was the most exotic creature that I had ever seen south of Wigan,' marvels Johnny Marr. 'I remember that he smelled really good.'

Dead Or Alive's Pete Burns hoved into view in a figure-hugging Vivienne Westwood lurid-yellow catsuit that led to a rehearsal phone call from *TOTP*'s producer to the costume depart-ment: 'He's moving around in his shorts too much – tape him down.' The wardrobe lady took one look at the singer and refused to go near him.

'It did look like I had a bag of onions down my crotch,' Burns was later to admit. 'But that's Vivienne Westwood for you.'

Chicks looked like guys, too. Annie Lennox and Grace Jones favoured masculine images through the 1980s, while the quiff-sporting, Elvis-impersonating Cher made a profound impact on Meat Loaf in 1995. 'If I had been a woman, I would have tried to pick her up,' he muses now.

Yet *TOTP*'s most legendary cross-dressing performance came in October 1982, when the then unknown Culture Club debuted 'Do You Really Want To Hurt Me?' 'We only got on *TOTP* because Shakin' Stevens was ill,' Boy George later confided. 'I probably owe my career to Shakin' Stevens.'

Arriving subdued and hungover, George vanished into his dressing room and emerged in inch-thick make-up and a long flowing smock-dress, his plaited hair festooned with bows. His performance propelled the song to No. 1 – and caused

It must be lobe: Rob Davis models a chandelier.

fevered debate up and down the land.

'If I had £10 for every time a bloke has come up to me and said, "I saw you on *TOTP* and I thought you were a bird", I'd be a rich man,' George was to reflect. 'Our plugger got called in and said, "We can't promote this! What is it – a bird, a plane, a drag queen?"'

'I was watching Culture Club

'My dad came in and said, "What the bloody hell's this? Is that a bloke?"'

Bob Stanley, St Etienne

on *TOTP* and my dad came in and said, "What the bloody hell's this? Is that a bloke?"' remembers Bob Stanley of St Etienne. 'I said, "Yeah, I think he looks great," and my dad said, "Oh, do you really? Would you like it if I came home dressed like that?" And I had to admit that, no, I really wouldn't.'

By George! A nation combusts.

A Dickhead In Love

In the kingdom of the blind, the one-eyed man is king. In a land where sorry sycophancy and gushing hyperbole are the norm, the man who speaks in a still, small voice of calm and reason shall be known as a prophet.

The late John Peel, Radio 1's resident 10pm to midnight black sheep, left an indelible mark on *TOTP* with his legendarily deadpan and ego-deflating hosting performances – and yet his debut on the show was toe-curlingly inauspicious.

Charged with introducing Amen Corner on a live 1968 show, Peel's mind went blank and he was left gulping at thin air as the baffled cameraman panned away to the band.

'This officious person walked over and told me that I'd never work in television again,' Peel later recounted. 'Frankly, I was delighted to hear it.'

Having made a slight return in 1971, miming playing the mandolin on 'Maggie May' for his mate Rod Stewart, Peel was surprisingly invited back into the *TOTP* fold in 1982, when the show was at its most garishly glitzy.

'I won't jump up and down like a Butlins Redcoat saying, "What a sensation!"' he warned producer Michael Hurll.

He was more than true to his word. Where others gushed,

> ## 'I won't jump up and down like a Butlins Redcoat saying, "What a sensation!"'
>
> **John Peel**

the understated Peel picked off the vainglorious with dry-witted ease, a loose cannon with the eye of a sniper. If *TOTP* was a live Thursday night party, Peel was the laconic bloke in the kitchen taking the piss.

On his return, he reintroduced himself to the nation: 'In case you're wondering who this funny old bloke is, I'm the one who comes on Radio 1 late at night and plays records by sulky Belgian art students in basements dying of TB.'

Peel mock-lauded an anodyne disco hit with a throwaway 'That record was the best thing since Napoleon's retreat from Moscow.' Yet he really hit his stride when he paired up with his Radio 1 'Rhythm Pal', David 'Kid' Jensen, to form a *TOTP* double act.

'Linx were on and David Grant was wearing a red leather jacket with big shoulders,' recalls Jensen. 'Peelie said, "Oh look, David's come as a fire hydrant." David looked livid.

'He introduced Toto as "those rock 'n' roll accountants" and, when we showed a Queen video shortly after they'd ignored sanctions and played South Africa in the apartheid era, John said, "Wa-hey! It's the Sun City Boys!"'

TOTP's Rhythm Pals shows quickly became a surrealist enclave of bizarre

Peel was a caustic and subversive presence.

running jokes and anti-showbiz mockery, with the earnest Kid playing the straight man to Peel's mordant wit. 'Wasn't that so good it made you want to spit?' asked Peel after Haysi Fantayzee's 'John Wayne Is Big Leggy', his face indicating the exact opposite.

'We would dress up as Robin Hood and his merry men, the Blues Brothers or Roman centurions,' recalls Jensen. 'We'd take it in turns to choose the costumes. Why did we do it? Absolutely no reason whatsoever.'

Peel's subversive spirit extended to his *TOTP* interviews. Given 15 seconds to ask Debbie Harry about her new single, he posed a question so long that she had no time to answer. The French balladeer Ryan Paris was notably

> ## 'This is the band that put the tree in Big Country.'
>
> **John Peel**

Lumberjacks: Big Country.

bemused to be asked, 'Do you change your name to a different European city every day? Tomorrow, will you be Ryan Münchengladbach?'

'I never tried to compete with John,' admits Jensen. 'The only time I was really taken aback was when he introduced Big Country by saying, "This is the band that put the tree in Big Country."'

'When Peelie said that, I thought, "Wow – how can you get away with saying that on BBC1 at 7.30pm?"' says an admiring Mike Read. 'But he seemed to manage it.'

In 1984, Kid Jensen quit Radio 1 and the BBC for Capital Radio and Peel cast around for a replacement: 'John asked me, "Can I host *TOTP* with you now?"' says Janice Long. 'He felt more comfortable doing it with somebody he knew. I was delighted.'

Peel and Long picked up where Peel and Jensen had left off. Introducing David Cassidy's comeback single 'The Last Kiss' in 1985, Long told her co-host: 'I had him on my bedroom wall when I was a teenager.' 'I never knew that you were so athletic, Janice,' replied Peel, just before she hit him.

A liberal spirit, Peel cared little for the music industry's casual sexism. When Robert Palmer showed up to *TOTP* with a backing troupe of scantily clad models to perform his lecherous 1986 hit 'Addicted To Love', Peel made his contempt clear: 'This is Robert Palmer, A Dickhead In Love.'

Aretha Franklin and George Michael fared little better with the following year's 'I Knew You Were Waiting For Me', despite making No. 1. 'You know, Aretha Franklin can make any old rubbish sound good,' Peel informed the nation, 'and I think she just has.'

Peel's incorrigible irreverence was infectious and Long was pleasingly keen to be led astray, making no attempt to hide her disdain when The Artist Formerly Known As Frank Spencer, the Broadway actor Michael Crawford, performed an orchestral show tune, 'The Music Of The

Kylie asks to borrow Peelie's Noseflutes 7".

Night', on *TOTP*.

'I said, "Well, I suppose *somebody* must like this record, for it to get in the Top 10",' she recalls. 'Quite a lot of people complained and Anne Robinson told us off on *Points of View*.'

Ironically, it was one of Peel's more innocuous comments that caused the largest furore in BBC circles. In May 1986, Peel and Long introduced their fellow Liverpudlian Pete Wylie singing the mid-chart single 'Sinful'. Adopting a novel tack, Peel told *TOTP* viewers: 'If that doesn't make No. 1, I'm going to come round and break wind in your kitchen.'

'Michael Hurll was in Australia at the time and was woken in the middle of the night and alerted to the extraordinary danger to national security engendered by me making this remark about breaking wind in people's kitchens,' Peel later marvelled. 'I thought that this was hilariously funny – not the remark, but the consequences of it.'

'We got told off – Peelie was deemed disgusting, and I was deemed irresponsible for laughing,' says Janice Long. 'But secretly Michael Hurll loved it and told us, "Do what you can to spice things up – phone calls mean people are watching."'

A beacon of flippant integrity in a shallow world, John Peel's sardonic turns were the best thing about *TOTP* for a certain school of mid-1980s cognoscenti. He left the programme's presentational roster early in 1987 and did so in typically maverick style.

'I was watching stock-car racing in Ipswich with my children,' he said later. 'This slightly drunk man came up to me and asked, "Oi, are you the bloke off the telly?"'

'I just thought, "No, I'm not really, I'm these kids' father." The idea of being the bloke off the telly seemed hugely unattractive. So I decided not to do it any more.'

> ## 'This is Robert Palmer, A Dickhead In Love.'
>
> ### John Peel

Blink And...
Oh, They've Gone

*T*OTP changed people's lives. For many artists, the BBC's weekly showcase proved a portal to vast fame and riches, a leg-up to a life of voluminous limos, eager groupies and stately-home residences that required their own postcode.

Others were not so lucky. For every Kylie, there was a Charlene, for every Craig David, an FR David – hapless tyros who burst onto *TOTP* and then vanished as quickly as they appeared.

The 1960s saw the Crazy World of Arthur Brown, Zager & Evans and the Overlanders all hit No. 1 but never trouble *TOTP*'s bookings agent again. Lee Marvin with 'Wand'rin' Star' and Clive Dunn with 'Grandad' were always going to be one-offs.

When the Royal Scots Dragoon Guards hit No. 1 with 'Amazing Grace' in 1972, the 68-strong platoon took their bagpipes to *TOTP*. Horrified at being kissed on the cheek by Jimmy Savile, their commanding officer trusted future interpretations to Pan's People.

TOTP was never likely to see a return visit by Canadian chancer JM Barrie, who hoved into view in 1976 looking like a Morecambe bingo caller to recite 'No Charge', a spoken-word homily backed by gospel caterwauling.

Three years later, US soul singer Anita Ward and Scottish crooner Lena Martell hoped to become *TOTP* regulars after No. 1s with 'Ring My Bell' and 'One Day At A Time' respectively. Neither was ever seen again.

In 1982, German Boney M-wannabes the Goombay Dance Band went the extra mile when they hit No. 1 with 'Seven Tears', hiring a fire-eater and handing out scarves to the entire *TOTP* audience. They really needn't have bothered.

The same year, US singer Charlene topped the chart with 'I've Never Been To Me', a song which laid claim to a life of debauched excess even though she appeared on *TOTP* looking as if she'd never left the house before.

The small children on stage with German electro-poppers Trio hinted that 1982's No. 2 'Da Da Da' might be a novelty hit. A year later, French balladeer FR David serenaded *TOTP* with 'Words' and then dried up.

Owen Paul hated his 1986 No. 3 'My Favourite Waste

The Clive Aid gig was ahead of its time.

Of Time' so much that he quit the music industry. He was last heard of living next door to the Osbournes.

In 1991, James debuted on *TOTP* with No. 2 'Sit Down', which was being held off the top slot by Chesney Hawkes' appropriately named 'The One And Only'.

'Chesney was embarrassed because he was a James fan and thought his own song was a bit of fluff,' bassist Jim Glennie recalled in the band's biography, *Folklore*. 'He came over to us really sheepishly and apologised.'

Despite singer Jas Mann proclaiming himself the future of music, Babylon Zoo never repeated the success of their 1996 No. 1 'Spaceman'. Four years later, indie band Black Box Recorder arrived at *TOTP* in a limo to play 'The Facts Of Life'.

'Our competition was two little-known teenagers: Britney Spears and Craig David,' the singer John Moore

> ## 'Chesney was embarrassed because he was a James fan and thought his own song was a bit of fluff.'
>
> **Jim Glennie, James**

Dr & the Medics fail to impress BUPA's marketing department.

later told the *Guardian* philosophically.

'Britney walked to her dressing room looking like a typical mall rat in fluffy jumper and plimsolls and emerged looking like something downloaded on Gary Glitter's computer.'

In 1970, the one-hit-wonder Norman Greenbaum hit No. 1 with 'Spirit In The Sky' then dematerialised. Ironically, the 1986 cover by Dr & the Medics shared exactly the same fate.

'Status Quo were on *TOTP* and Francis Rossi asked me, "Why did you cover that song?"' remembers singer Clive Jackson.

'I said, "It wasn't a bad choice – we're No. 1 and you're No. 27!" He smiled, tapped me on the shoulder and said, "Oh well, son, only another 32 hits to go."

'I suppose he was right.'

Friend Or Foe

You hang with the most incongruous people on package holidays. Shoved into a random, temporary new social circle, you spend a week getting hammered every night with the nice young couple of legal clerks from Stoke-on-Trent who are staying in the next chalet.

Similar dynamics applied at *TOTP*, where everybody from Elton John to Jilted John had a day to kill at Television Centre and the unlikeliest new friendships – or enmities – were formed.

'The Damned spent hours drinking with Elkie Brooks,' recalls Rat Scabies. 'She was so cool and bought us loads of bottles of champagne.'

'We'd get pissed with Mud or Status Quo, but the band who really were mad as fucking hatters were Boney M,' says Noddy Holder. 'They were always up for a party and I don't just mean drink. We used to have a right riot when they were around.'

> ## 'We had a lovely chat with Bing and his mate Fred Astaire. They were a laid-back pair of gentlemen.'
>
> ### Dave Bartram, Showaddywaddy

Regarded as the 'house band' in their imperial period at *TOTP*, Slade emerged as the life and soul of the 1970s Thursday night party to which everybody appeared to be invited.

'We took the Osmonds to Tramp on their first visit,' says Noddy. 'They all came except Donny, who had to go to bed. They had never been to a nightclub before and didn't drink, but they seemed to enjoy it.'

'That was always happening!' Donny complains, scratching an old sore. 'My brothers would go out but I would be told, "You can't go." I used to figure, "What the heck?"'

Some weeks *TOTP* would fall into its usual backstage routine of being a VIP social club with a constantly shifting membership list. On other occasions, artists sensed greatness in their midst and got a rare chance to mingle with musical legends.

'During rehearsals, the artists would be on their podiums

Boney M: it's always the quiet ones.

Tramp had a strict dress policy: smart-casual or panto freak-show.

and the cameras would zoom between us as we practised,' remembers Cilla Black.

'One week Stevie Wonder was on the next podium to me. He heard me rehearsing and shouted out that he knew who I was and thought I had a wonderful voice. It meant so much to me and it still does when I think about it now.'

'I saw Bryan Ferry in the toilet, having a wee,' divulges Gary Numan. 'I wanted to say hello to him, but you don't really in the toilet, do you?

'Then a few months later I met him again, on a TV show in Germany, but unfortunately that was in the toilet, as well.'

Cliff Richard speaks fondly of the happy camaraderie between artists waiting to do their *TOTP* turn, but this fellow feeling was arguably in short supply when he appeared on the show's 500th edition in 1973 along with The Who.

Less than ardent fans of Cliff's clean-cut rock, Keith Moon and The Who's stage crew raided a BBC costume cupboard for a stash of wigs, which they then frisbeed at the Bachelor Boy as he began performing his number.

'It was one of those funny, crazy, stupid things,' reckons

Cliff. 'It was very rock 'n' roll – I was trying to sing and wigs were just flying everywhere!

'I didn't mind because it wasn't aggressive and they weren't throwing them at me, they were throwing them into my performance. Hey – at least they weren't throwing chairs!'

'We met Simon & Garfunkel at *TOTP*,' says Reg Presley of the Troggs. 'We sat at a table and had a nice sandwich together.' Yet this encounter was dwarfed in July 1975 when a bona fide Hollywood A-lister fetched up in White City.

On *TOTP* to perform his (flop) single 'That's What Life Is All About', Bing Crosby chewed the cud with former Prime Minister Edward Heath, who was at the BBC to record an interview with Robin Day.

Then he aimed his conversational sights higher: to Showaddywaddy. 'We had a lovely chat with Bing and his mate Fred Astaire,' says Dave Bartram. 'They were a laid-back pair of gentlemen. My dad was very envious.'

Remarkably, even this meeting appeared positively prosaic next to one Christmas *TOTP* match-up. 'We were thrilled to get the chance to talk to Bob Marley,' muses Tommy Banner of the Wurzels. 'I assume he felt the same.'

'When we were on *TOTP*,

Bryan Ferry battles that 'bursting bladder' feeling.

Bob Marley contemplates a toke and a zider.

I spent all my time getting autographs for my daughter,' admits Strawbs singer Dave Cousins. 'I remember Errol Brown from Hot Chocolate signing one with his trousers round his ankles.'

'The coolest people were the ones you least expected,' notes Rat Scabies. Andy McCluskey, singer for Orchestral Manoeuvres in the Dark, shares the Damned drummer's view that it was wisest to leave your character preconceptions in Wood Lane.

'Even people whose music you absolutely loathed and despised turned out to be quite nice in person,' he confesses.

'When you are a precocious, pretentious young person, you say things like, "I hate Status Quo, they are fucking shit." Then you meet them and think, "Oh, they're all right, aren't they?"'

'When Bucks Fizz were at our peak, Paul McCartney asked us for our autographs on *TOTP*,' says Cheryl Baker. 'He said that it was for his daughter, which must have been Stella. It's funny, she never mentions it now.

'Victoria Beckham told me at *TOTP* that, when she was a little girl, we were her favourite band. We also often hung out with the Human League. Suzanne was always good fun.'

'Yes, she was,' agrees Cheryl's band mate, Mike Nolan. 'A lot more than bloody Nena.'

Post-punk, demarcation lines were drawn in the musical sand, and leftfield artists began to apply stringent ideological criteria to decide whom to socialise with. Some used their *TOTP* trips to strike a militant blow against the mainstream.

'We went round the BBC with black marker pens drawing moustaches on the photos of cheesy famous Scousers on the walls,' says Keith Mullen of the Farm. 'It was our form of art rebellion.'

'The Smiths had a *TOTP* rule that we wouldn't hang out with anybody if we didn't like their music,' recalls Johnny Marr. 'We thought it would be hypocritical.

'The only exception was when Nick Heyward from

> '**When Buck/ Fizz were at our peak, Paul McCartney a/ked u/ for our autograph/ on TOTP.'**
>
> **Cheryl Baker**

Haircut 100 barged into our dressing room, picked up my guitar and played "Stairway To Heaven" to us on it. He was so funny that we ended up liking him.'

'The Wedding Present had a great chat with Jason Donovan but we were shocked at how much he kept swearing,' says David Gedge. However, not all of the expletives that were heard backstage were quite so affable.

Rock stars have large egos and short attention spans, *TOTP* was a highly competitive environment and every now and then musicians inevitably found themselves at loggerheads.

> ## 'The Wedding Present had a great chat with Jason Donovan, but we were shocked at how much he kept swearing.'
>
> **David Gedge**

'The *NME* had asked me to review some singles and I hadn't been very complimentary about Elvis Costello's new record,' recalls Glenn Gregory of Heaven 17.

'He buttonholed me at *TOTP* and went on about it for ages. I was saying, "Look, mate, I'm sorry, I don't like the song!" But he just wouldn't shut up.'

Even Slade, glam rock's reliable good time that was had by all, fell victim to some post-show BBC bar joshing that turned into a bout of fisticuffs.

'Ray Davies from the Kinks came up to us and said, "Don't keep doing the same thing",' their bassist Jim Lea recounted.

'The Wurzels meet Bob Marley and I get bloody Bucks Fizz …'

Elvis Costello sings a song that nobody could possibly dislike.

'We did *TOTP* with Madonna in 1997 and she stayed sequestered in her room the entire time,' regrets Katrina Leskanich of Katrina & the Waves. 'We kept walking past just to get a waft of her incredibly expensive perfume.

'She had a maid with her, holding baby Lourdes, and we tried to play with her because we figured, if we couldn't get anywhere near Madonna, at least we could touch her baby.'

Madonna's fellow 1980s titan Prince also made a rare trip to *TOTP* in the show's dying days and, in trademark style, insisted that the artists' backstage communal relaxation room should be cleared before he would even contemplate passing through it.

'Prince had this huge entourage with him and we were all told that nobody should talk to him or look him in the eye, and the entire set had to be cleared for his rehearsal,' explains Fran Healy of Travis.

'Robbie Williams was on the show and objected hugely to all this, so when he went on to do his song, he proceeded to yell swear words left, right and centre as he told the audience what an absolute arse Prince was being.

'The best bit was when he started singing, "*Tonight I'm gonna kick somebody's head in like it's 1999*". The crowd absolutely loved it.'

Yet when it came to being exotically aloof, even Prince could have learned from Britain's master of the barbed snub.

'Inspiral Carpets were on the same *TOTP* as Morrissey and we stood by him in a corridor waiting to go on,' says Clint Boon. 'We were dying to talk to him and kept trying to make eye contact but he wouldn't even glance at us.

'I was gutted … but it was just Morrissey being Morrissey.'

'I hummed some of his hits at him and said, "Why not? It never stopped you!" He threw his Coca-Cola over me and it all kicked off. We were banned from the Television Centre bar for months.'

Most pop stars who visited *TOTP* refrained from coming to blows, but this didn't mean everybody wanted to join the big backstage social shindig. Even the best parties have their wallflowers.

'David Soul had a hit while we were on *TOTP* and I watched him come out of his dressing room to do his rehearsal,' says Jet Black from the Stranglers.

'He was surrounded by three heavies who linked arms and walked sideways like crabs to shelter him from the masses, even though nobody who was there had any interest in him whatsoever.'

'David Bowie came on *TOTP* so we were all really excited but he brought these two bodyguards with him who looked like Sumo wrestlers,' remembers Janice Long.

'They sat outside his dressing room, which was next door to mine, and every time I went in or out of my room, they leapt up as if they were going to attack me.'

Football managers routinely parrot that no player is bigger than the team. In sharp contrast, later-period *TOTP* received visitations from some of music's biggest prima donnas who *knew* that, not only were they far bigger than the show, but the show was lucky to have them.

> **'David Bowie came on *TOTP* but he brought two bodyguards who looked like Sumo wrestlers.'**
>
> **Janice Long**

Morrissey: went and stood on his own, and left on his own.

Frankly Disgusting

The BBC was founded in 1922 with a remit to be both a broadcasting service and a guardian of national morals. Its Presbyterian founder, Lord Reith, famously once banned a divorcée from playing the violin on the radio.

Old habits die hard and over the years *TOTP* drew a red line through copious tracks that offended the Beeb's sense of decency – a salutary reminder that another of its nicknames, 'Auntie', was short for 'Auntie knows best'.

TOTP looked askance at the Rolling Stones' promiscuity-encouraging 'Let's Spend The Night Together' and believed the sound at the end of the Troggs' 'I Can't Control Myself' suggested Reg Presley orgasming, which they felt nobody would want to see. They were probably right.

Jane Birkin and Serge Gainsbourg's 1969 No. 1 'Je T'Aime… Moi Non Plus' also fell foul of the censors. Rightly so, reckons Jimmy Savile: 'Goodness gracious, *TOTP* could not play all that sexy breathing! Oioioioioi!'

Paul McCartney and Wings' 1972 hit 'Give Ireland Back To The Irish' was always going to be banned

Frankie's Holly Johnson demonstrates the Power of Glove.

After the copious protests about the Prodigy's video for 'Firestarter', the band could hardly expect *TOTP* to give house room to 'Smack My Bitch Up'. Yet the show's most infamous banning was Frankie Goes To Hollywood's enormous 1984 No. 1 'Relax'.

Frankie had already played 'Relax' on *TOTP* before its lascivious homosexual innuendo came to the attention of Mike Read on his Radio 1 breakfast programme.

'I glanced at the sleeve,' explains Read. 'It said, "Go down on me baby and lick the shit off my shoes", and there was a phallus. My producer said he'd found his kids rewinding the video. It had a man urinating off a balcony into someone's mouth, and simulated buggery.'

Read refused to play the 'obscene' song on air and a BBC

but the censoring of Rod Stewart's 'Tonight's The Night' was more puzzling. Judge Dread's string of innuendo-laden 1970's white reggae hits ('Big Six, Big Seven', etc.) also never made it to White City.

Punk brought a rash of BBC vetoes, including the Sex Pistols' 'God Save The Queen', No. 2 during the Queen's silver jubilee week. The Police's video for their 1981 Northern Ireland-focused single 'Invisible Sun' was deemed 'too political'.

Heaven 17's debut single '(We Don't Need This) Fascist Groove Thing' was nixed on similar grounds. 'We said we'd never play *TOTP* after that,' admits Glenn Gregory. 'Of course, we couldn't stay away.'

The second summer of love in 1988 saw D-Mob's No. 3 'We Call It Acieeed' given the red card after Peter Powell delivered a Reithian moral homily on Radio 1: 'acid house is near to mass organised zombiedom – I don't think it should go any further'.

> ## 'I glanced at the [Relax] sleeve. It said, "Go down on me baby and lick the shit off my shoes", and there was a phallus.'
>
> ### Mike Read

ban followed. Pop fans reacted by buying nearly two million copies. 'Relax' was No. 1 for five weeks, during which *TOTP* climaxed with the chart No. 2.

'I thought it was hypocrisy for *TOTP* to play it then ban it,' Holly Johnson of Frankie later reflected. 'We used it in our ads: "Big, Banned and Beautiful".

'Then they sheepishly said, "We'll let you do 'Relax' on Christmas *TOTP*." We said, "Really? Why couldn't we do it all year, then?" I just thought it was foolish.'

'Look, I didn't ban "Relax",' insists Mike Read. 'I was a BBC employee; I couldn't ban anything. But even now, if I walk into a disco, the DJ puts it on. People expect me to go mad. They are amazed when I start dancing to it.

'There have been so many stories, including that I punched Holly, but I love the song – I even did a voiceover for Frankie's album! Oh, and also…'

It's OK, Mike. Relax. Don't do it.

Heaven 17: 'We're never playing this show again … oh, go on, then.'

Booze Sorry Now?

A hard taskmaster, *TOTP* routinely required artists to turn up at Television Centre at 10am and stay put for 12 hours. In that time, they had one camera rehearsal, one dress rehearsal, one mimed performance ... and eleven-and-a-half hours of nothing.

It's probably no surprise that *TOTP* developed a serious drinking culture.

'Our record label would give us loads of booze and we'd drink all day,' recalls Noddy Holder fondly. 'Our dressing room was always the party room.

'We knew all the drinkers, like Mud and the Quo. We didn't see a lot of Cliff.'

'Black Lace had an ambition to do *TOTP* sober but we never managed it,' admits Colin Gibb. 'Mind you, with the kind of stuff we had to play, being drunk helped.'

Unknown to the BBC, alcohol was frequently only part of the story. White City's corridors were full of wayward souls firmly of the opinion that The Drugs *Do* Work.

'We got to *TOTP* and Lemmy from Motorhead was there with his Swiss Army knife and a big bag of speed,' says Francis Rossi. 'He said, "Do you want a line, lads?"

'I said, "It's a bit early for us, Lem", and he said, "OK, do you want some orange juice? It's got vodka and a gram

of speed in it." I said, "A gram? It's 10 in the morning!"'

'You did so much hanging around at *TOTP* that we used to take Frustration in with us to play,' remembers Wayne Hussey of The Mission.

'Apart from rehearsal and performance, we'd spend the entire day in our dressing room drinking, doing speed and playing Frustration.'

'We only got on *TOTP* once,' noted Jim Reid of mid-1980s indie noiseniks The Jesus & Mary Chain. 'We were nervous and, to us, nervous equals drunk.

'We had a few cans in the *Blue Peter* garden and I was astounded that nobody seemed to mind these alcoholic rock 'n' roll types stumbling around a kids' TV set.'

With only a mimed performance over recorded playback awaiting them at the end of the day, artists had no reason to stint on the partying. Nevertheless, backstage excesses made for some memorable on-screen mishaps.

> ## 'We knew all the drinkers, like Mud and the Quo. We didn't see a lot of Cliff.'
>
> **Noddy Holder**

Black Lace: lager helped to kill the pain.

Shane McGowan's famously paralytic 1991 performance of 'Fairy Tale Of New York' that ended with the Pogues singer collapsing into his band's drum kit.

'Just before the Pogues went on, I was watching Shane in the canteen,' recalls Richard Fairbrass of Right Said Fred.

'He was staggering around and around the cheese counter, trying to work out what to eat, and he was absolutely three sheets to the wind.'

'I remember getting to *TOTP*, seeing Teardrop Explodes and going over to say hello to Julian Cope,' remembers Andy McCluskey of OMD.

'The conversation never really got started, but that was because he was standing on top of a piano in his bare feet, off his face on acid.'

'I sang "What" in 1982 completely off my head, wearing a dreadful hat and with chicken bones around my neck,' confesses Soft Cell singer Marc Almond.

'It was a live show and the studio was spinning around so badly that I thought I was going to be sick and fall over in front of millions of people on television. I can never watch that performance again. The very thought of it fills me with dread.'

It's no great surprise that the punk and New Romantic eras were times of clandestine narcotic excess at *TOTP*, but Britpop bands were also no slackers in the hedonistic stakes.

'There was a time in the mid-1990s when everybody

In 1976, sub-glam pop band Sailor performed a squiffy mime to 'One Drink Too Many'. It was the birthday of the singer Georg Kajanus and they had taken their own advice literally.

'When we did "The Cutter" in 1982, we hadn't managed to switch our backing tape so we had to mime to this crappy version that was like a demo,' recalls Ian McCulloch, singer with Echo & the Bunnymen.

'I was so angry that I went to the bar and got bladdered. When we did our performance, I pulled my t-shirt right down to show my chest. It looked weird but great – even Paul McCartney mentioned it to me.'

This was nothing next to

> ## 'We'd spend the entire day in our dressing room drinking, doing speed and playing Frustration.'
>
> **Wayne Hussey, The Mission**

who went on *TOTP* was drunk,' Blur bassist Alex James nostalgically reflected.

'But when we were on in the show's later years, it was full of very young people whose minders wouldn't let them near the bar, which was a shame.'

'We came back off a long tour once and did *TOTP* and I was totally out there,' remembers Supergrass drummer Danny Goffey.

'I had a long black coat on and was rocking back and forwards like a mental patient.

'A few years later, I saw it again on *TOTP2*, and Steve Wright said, "Just have a look at the drummer – he's definitely been up to no good."'

After a long day's indulgence backstage, the truly dedicated party people attempted to prolong the session post-filming in the BBC bar.

'The BBC bar was fantastic,' sighs Glenn Tilbrook of Squeeze. 'There would be people from *I, Claudius* wandering past in togas, having a quick half of bitter and a Scotch.'

'Lemmy loved it,' says Rat Scabies, 'because it had a big pay-out on the one-armed bandit.'

This establishment had mixed feelings towards its musical guests, often with good reason. Refused admission by a BBC commissionaire in 1973, Keith Moon, drummer of The Who, promptly attacked him.

'I went up to the bar and one of the doormen had two black eyes,' Cherry Gillespie of Pan's People later reported. 'I asked him, "What happened?"

'He pointed at one of them and said "Keith Moon" and at the other and said "Marty Feldman".'

Yet the biggest threat to the health and safety of the BBC's employees came not from any of rock's wild men or speed freaks, but from a group of purportedly harmless West Country zider drinkers.

'The first time the Wurzels did *TOTP*, we took a five-gallon barrel of real scrumpy and a big stack of plastic cups with us,' says Tommy Banner. 'Just to be sociable, like.

'Some of the BBC office girls and secretaries knew it was our first visit so they came in our dressing room to wish us luck. We offered them some cider. They hadn't had

Mud's Les Gray: you'd need beer goggles.

scrumpy before and they were saying, "Ooh, that's nice, can I have another one?"

'We went back two weeks later and took another barrel. The same girls came in to wish us luck again but, when we offered them another drink, they said, "Oh, no, thank you."

'Apparently one of them hadn't even made it home after work the last time because she fell asleep on the train and woke up at the end of the line, not knowing where she was.

'Another girl spent the night in a police cell because they found her collapsed in a hedge, covered in sick. Maybe we should have warned them.'

'There would be people from I, Claudius wandering past in togas, having a quick half of bitter and a Scotch.'

Glenn Tilbrook, Squeeze

'They don't understand our country ways!'

Freaky Dancing

Pop historians often pronounce that the Madchester indie-dance scene arrived on *TOTP* on November 23, 1989, when the Stone Roses and Happy Mondays loped on to the same show to play 'Fool's Gold' and 'Hallelujah!' respectively. Pop historians are wrong.

Bez, the Happy Mondays' freaky dancer and a man of a thousand gurns, had spent 1988 gobbling pills and perfecting his loose-limbed shuffle at the New Order-owned Hacienda club in Manchester.

Like John the Baptist preceding Christ, when New Order went on *TOTP* with 'Fine Time' that December, singer Bernard Sumner aped Bez's soon-to-be-infamous orang-utan-on-Ecstasy strut. He looked bonkers.

'Bernard was impersonating Bez, but he was also doing what he did himself every night,' reflects Johnny Marr. 'It was an incredible performance, demented and very druggy – a blow for the underground. Frankly, it was jaw-droppingly subversive.'

After this idiosyncratic sneak preview, *TOTP* got the real deal the following November when Ian Brown pimp-rolled through a loose mime of 'Fool's Gold', having been refused permission to sing live. It was probably for the best. Kirsty MacColl joined Happy Mondays for 'Hallelujah!'

The baggy rock Messiahs had been chosen – but it could have been so different.

'A few weeks earlier we released a single called "Move" and it went in the charts at No. 49,' remembers Clint Boon of Inspiral Carpets. 'We had been told that if it went Top 40 we would definitely get *TOTP* and then we'd have been the first Madchester band on the show.

'It was frustrating for us to come so close, but it was brilliant because it was the moment the nation switched on and realised something big was happening in Manchester.'

Never one to miss a blag, Shaun Ryder demanded new threads for the show. Happy Mondays' label, Factory Records, stumped up £1,000 for each band member: 'We spent about £300 and pocketed the rest,' recalled Shaun's brother and Mondays' guitarist, Paul Ryder.

For their part, the Stone Roses were delighted to arrive at Television Centre and discover that the décor was reassuringly familiar.

'The BBC is run by the Government,' Ian Brown, a man who has always been partial to a good conspiracy theory, later explained to the *Guardian*. 'So it means that all the dressing rooms at Television Centre are exactly the same as the ones you go to when you are signing on, or when the DHSS call you in for a meeting.'

With the traditional long hours to fill before wowing the nation, the two bands settled down for a chilled afternoon of toking and plotting.

'We were all pretty heavily sedated,' Paul Ryder reflected later. 'I vividly remember sitting in the BBC garden and Shaun and Ian were chuckling and planning to swap drummers. I think the BBC rumbled it.

'To be honest, we never realised at the time that us and the Stone Roses appearing on the same *TOTP* would become a seminal moment. But, when we got back up to Manchester, people told us that all the bars had set up screens especially to watch it, so it was a big deal.'

And what of Madchester's wild-eyed, jiggling talisman? Are the seismic, life-altering events of 23/11/89 still etched deeply in his cranium as if it were yesterday? No, not exactly.

'I can't remember much about the day, but I think we mimed,' mused Bez, a man to whom history will always be bunk. 'The singing might have been live, but I wouldn't swear to that, either.'

> ## 'Frankly, it was jaw-droppingly subversive.'
>
> ### Johnny Marr

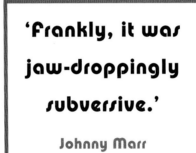

'I can't remember much about the day,' admits Bez.

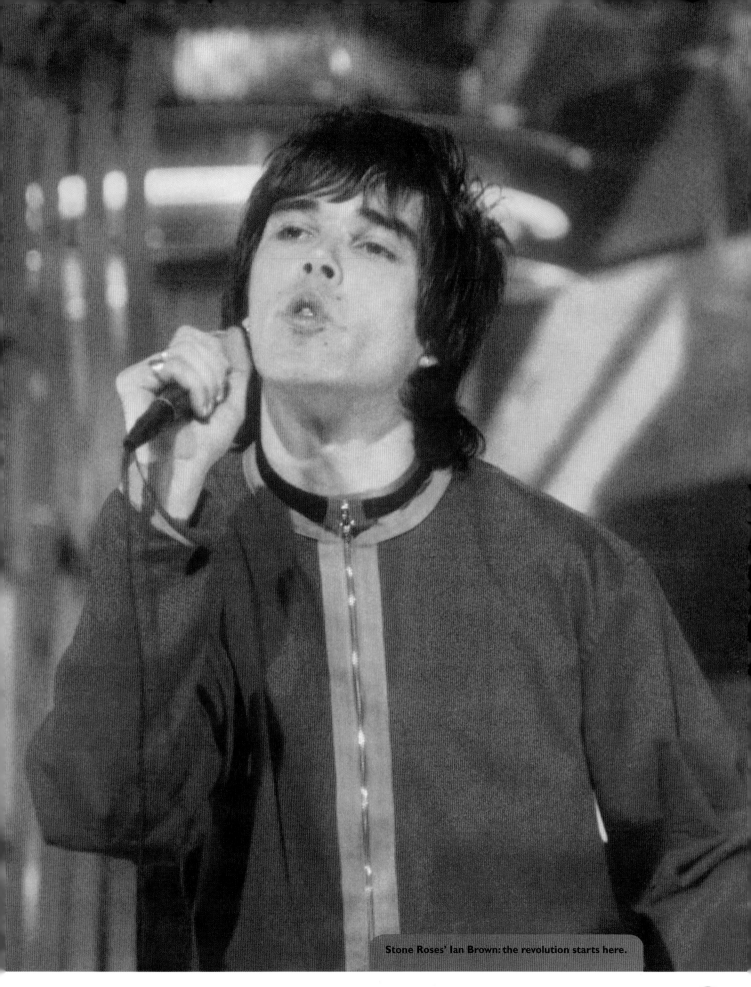

Stone Roses' Ian Brown: the revolution starts here.

Lips Don't Lie (Oh, Yes They Do!)

No other topic in *TOTP*'s colourful history has proved as contentious as the perennial question: to mime, or not to mime?

Over the programme's 42-year run, its producers tried every possible combination of performance options. Artists mimed to records, sang live with orchestras, did live vocals over pre-recorded backing tapes, did the whole thing live and went back to miming again.

Noddy Holder had no doubts of his preferred *modus operandi*.

'I liked singing live over backing tapes,' he says. 'That way we could drink all day, then put on a great performance without having to worry about playing music.'

The show's early Manchester years saw all the artists miming to their records spun by disc maid Samantha Juste, and *TOTP* sage Jimmy Savile saw no problem with this system.

'If you had somebody like Freddie Garrity of Freddie and the Dreamers, his game was springing about the stage, and he couldn't do that and sing at the same time,' he explains. 'So I saw no reason why bands shouldn't mime.'

After the Musicians Union's intervention when the show moved to London, the system switched to artists miming to pre-recorded backing tapes. The vast majority were happy to do this, while exploiting any opportunity for high jinks.

When The Who played the *TOTP* New Year's Eve special in 1990, Viv Stanshall of the Bonzo Dog Doo Dah Band stood behind Keith Moon, pulling a rope attached to the drummer's right wrist every time the camera was on him.

Rod Stewart was even more cavalier. When the bassist Ronnie Lane was absent from a 1972 *TOTP* performance of 'Angel', Stewart stood a cardboard cut-out in his place.

'One band called 5000 Volts had a 1975 hit called "I'm On Fire" and their lead singer was a girl called Tina Charles,' remembers David Hamilton.

Like all great singers, Noddy performed best after a skinful.

Kursaal Flyers behaved like silly suds.

'Tina was slightly plump and not terribly visual, so when they came on *TOTP* they brought a different front girl, called Linda Kelly, who mimed to Tina's voice.'

'I went on *TOTP* twice singing "I'm A Believer" and used different musicians both times for a laugh,' says Robert Wyatt. 'Andy Summers and Nick Mason pretended to play.'

Yet in this area, as in so many others, punk was to prove a major tipping-point. Hooked on authenticity, late 1970s bands professed their disdain for this 'phoney' element of the show, with The Clash citing it as the main reason for their boycott of the programme.

Less fundamentalist punk and new wave bands bit the bullet and went on *TOTP* but made it clear they felt that miming was a sham.

> '**We could drink all day, then put on a great performance without having to worry about playing music.**'
>
> *Noddy Holder*

For 1977's 'No More Heroes', the Stranglers' Hugh Cornwell 'played' his guitar with his teeth while Jet Black faced away from his kit and drummed thin air. On 'Little Does She Know', Southend pub rockers the Kursaal Flyers plugged their guitars into giant packets of soap powder rather than amps.

'I remember seeing The Police on *TOTP* as a kid and Sting sang into a banana instead of a microphone,' says Richard Fairbrass. 'I was inordinately impressed by that.'

'Madness would be on *TOTP* and our saxophonist, Lee, would be chewing gum when he was supposed to be doing his solo,' singer Suggs divulged.

'Michael Hurll would tear down from the gallery to tell us, "You're an embarrassment to yourselves and the BBC." I

New Order single-handedly killed the Keep Music Live campaign.

almost expected him to add, "… and the Queen."'

Not everybody obeyed the *TOTP* diktat on miming. New Order insisted on playing their monster electronic hit 'Blue Monday' completely live. It was not to be their finest hour.

'The *TOTP* engineers spent hours putting "BBC-approved" stickers on all our plugs,' drummer Stephen Morris recalled. '"Blue Monday" was never the easiest song to play and we made a complete balls of it. The synthesizers went awry. It sounded awful.'

'It didn't help,' says an admiring Johnny Marr, who watched the live performance, 'when Stephen made a mistake halfway through and Bernard burst out laughing.'

Billy Bragg won plaudits for

his 1985 *TOTP* debut when he played 'Between The Wars' live on an acoustic guitar. Three years later, his return was less auspicious.

'I had a double A-side No. I charity record for five weeks with Wet Wet Wet,' he says. 'They sang "With A Little Help From My Friends" and I did "She's Leaving Home". *TOTP* had Wet Wet Wet on for four weeks in a row, then my record company finally persuaded them to let me on.

'I insisted on playing live, which pissed them off, and they were even more annoyed when I realised I didn't know the lyrics very well: when I'd recorded it, I'd had them in front of me in the studio. So *TOTP* taped the words on the floor by my feet.

'As soon as I started singing,

> **'I insisted on playing live, which pissed them off, and they were even more annoyed when I realised I didn't know the lyrics very well.'**
>
> **Billy Bragg**

I heard this hissing noise and all this dry ice swirled around me. Normally it floats off but this was really expensive BBC *Hound of the Baskervilles* dry ice. It stayed thick up to my knees.

'I was singing and desperately kicking my left foot in the air, trying to clear the dry ice to read the lyrics, when this

'Some hairy technician guy down the front said to me, "Sing something!"'

Julianne Regan, All About Eve

All About Eve sink in 'Martha's Harbour'.

bloke in brown overalls walked behind the crowd carrying a 10-foot ladder and dropped it with a resounding crash. The audience all looked round to see what the noise was.

'I finished, and to my utter amazement the director said, "Yeah, that's a take." I couldn't believe it. The next night, I watched it on TV at my mum's with my head in my hands. It was bloody awful.'

At least Bragg was partly to blame for his own downfall. Wistful art-goths All About Eve were utterly blameless when a live 1988 appearance turned into spectacular car-crash TV.

Waiting to mime to 'Martha's Harbour', singer Julianne Regan and guitarist Tim Bricheno sat blank-faced and motionless on stools as the song chimed out of the nation's TV sets.

'We waited to hear the first couple of notes so we could start miming,' Regan later told the *Guardian*. 'We heard nothing at all, then some hairy technician guy down the front said to me, "Sing something!"

'It seemed to go on for minutes but it was about 30 seconds, then suddenly the monitor in front of me kicked in and I started singing. It turned out some technician had tripped and pulled a lead out of a socket.

'Afterwards Janice Long and Mark Goodier came to our dressing room and offered condolences as if there had been some kind of death. There must have been a big sympathy vote because the song went up five places the next week.'

A few diligent, image-aware artists looked to perfect the art of miming. Spandau Ballet were among them. 'I always told Tony Hadley to sing even if we were miming,' says Gary Kemp. 'Otherwise, people would see his larynx wasn't moving properly.'

However, far more acts seized the opportunity for a gentle piss-take. When Marillion's Fish had laryngitis when he was due to perform 'Lavender' in 1985, he held up the lyrics on a blackboard and got the studio audience to sing them for him.

The Cure dressed their guitars in clothes and 'played' them left-handed, while Ian McCulloch of Echo & the Bunnymen had his own narcissistic agenda.

'I figured that if I kept my gob fairly shut and didn't move my lips too much, I would look like I did in photos,' he reveals. 'And I looked mega in photos.'

> **'If you want us to sing live, we want paying.'**
>
> **Noel Gallagher**

Big Country drummer Mark Brzezicki showed masterly improvisation. Realising he had forgotten his sticks ten seconds before the band's live slot, he banged his drums with a hammer that he grabbed from a workman standing by the stage.

'When we played "Deliverance" on *TOTP* in 1990, I stood six feet from the mic and didn't even bother trying to mime,' says The Mission singer Wayne Hussey.

'The producer wasn't very happy but the programme was going out live, so there was nothing he could do.'

Mike Patton, the vocalist of the US metal band Faith No More showed he was miming by sticking his tongue out during close-up shots. EMF took to the stage with their guitarist sporting boxing gloves, while Eels played plastic toy instruments, which they then trashed.

'We had a double-necked guitar, but one neck was a

'Sing live? Do you think we're dumb?'

Supergrass. Plant-loving drummer thankfully not pictured.

lead guitar and one was a bass,' says The Wedding Present singer, David Gedge. 'That was great because it was the kind of thing only other musicians would notice.'

For 1995's 'Charmless Man', Blur's Graham Coxon strummed a miniature guitar while Dave Rowntree wielded giant drumsticks. Their Britpop nemesis Oasis took things much further.

On 'Whatever', rhythm guitarist Bonehead sawed at a cello in the symphony orchestra as the female cellist mimed playing his guitar. For 'Lyla', Liam Gallagher chewed gum and walked away from the mic as his distinctive vocal echoed round the studio.

'TOTP would always ask us, "Do you want to sing live?"' Noel divulged. 'And I'd say, "Fuck that. If you want us to sing live, we want paying."

'We were very happy getting pissed in the bar, knowing that we only had to mime on the programme.'

'I sent one of the BBC runners out to buy some rhubarb, because I decided I really wanted to play the drums with sticks of rhubarb on *TOTP*,' remembers Supergrass drummer Danny Goffey.

> **'I sent one of the BBC runners out to buy some rhubarb, because I decided I really wanted to play the drums with sticks of rhubarb on *TOTP*.'**
>
> **Danny Goffey, Supergrass**

'They were gone for two hours and then came back really upset because they hadn't been able to find any. So I made two really weird sticks out of a mop instead.'

In its final years, *TOTP* once again made it compulsory for artists to play live, in a doomed attempt to reintroduce greater edge and urgency to the show. Dogged traditionalists at heart, one of the most inspirational bands ever to grace the programme found this decision hugely disappointing.

'Morrissey and I thought that when the Smiths went on *TOTP*, we should always mime and he should try to make a couple of lip-synching mistakes,' reveals Johnny Marr. 'That was how Marc Bolan had done it.'

Such reverence for rock history is laudable, but the Wurzels had an even more legitimate reason for Keeping It Real.

'We always insisted that we did live vocals on *TOTP*,' claims accordionist and pianist Tommy Banner. 'Our singer, Pete, used to shout, "Ooh arr!" a lot between the verses and he said that he would feel silly miming them.'

Who Are You?

It was a truly Herculean challenge to dumb down *TOTP*. Somehow, in the late 1980s, the BBC managed it.

Since it launched in 1967, Radio 1 had had a symbiotic relationship with *TOTP*. The radio DJs were also the BBC's TV faces of pop. It was a cosy relationship and, like all cosy things, nicely familiar.

Yet in 1988, possibly reacting to the tirelessly fresh-faced MTV, the show's producers decided to cut the umbilical cord. The rolled-up sleeves of Mike Read, Steve Wright, Mike Smith and Peter Powell were suddenly no longer required.

In their place, the bosses airlifted in a motley crop of BBC kids' TV presenters: Anthea Turner, Andy Crane, Caron Keating, Jenny Powell, Simon Parkin and Andi Peters (minus his Orville-like sidekick, Edd the Duck).

'For some reason, they started introducing little blondes

> ## 'For some reason, they started introducing little blondes from children's programmes.'
>
> ### Tony Blackburn

from children's programmes,' sniffs Tony Blackburn. 'I just thought, "They're not really music people."'

TOTP kept a few of the fresher Radio 1 faces such as Simon Mayo, Nicky Campbell and Mark Goodier. However, with the show going out live, the sticky-back-plastic brigade inevitably produced a string of on-screen howlers.

In June 1989, R.E.M. debuted on *TOTP* with 'Orange Crush'. It was a typically spectral, tangential song about the US military's use of Agent Orange in Vietnam, but its subtleties were lost on Simon Parkin: 'Mmm!' he grinned inanely. 'Lovely on a hot summer's day!'

David Gedge of indie stalwarts The Wedding Present had dreamed of appearing on *TOTP* since he was a boy. At no point had his dream included being introduced by a ludicrously perky Anthea Turner off *Blue Peter* in a shiny blue leather jacket.

'She said, "This is The Wedding Present. I'll have a

The showbiz razzmatazz of The Wedding Present.

And you are? Left to right: Adrian Rose, Femi Oke and Claudia Simon.

toaster please, ha ha!"' he winces, his pain clearly still not fully healed nearly 20 years on. 'It was absolutely meaningless and totally unfunny.'

Early in 1991, Anthea rebranded art pranksters The KLF as KLM – the Dutch national airline. 'I wasn't allowed to go back and change it,' she said afterwards. 'Still, I suppose it was a great advert for them!'

'It was awful,' recalls St Etienne's Bob Stanley. 'At least you could despise the Radio 1 DJs and go to school the next day and say, "Isn't DLT a complete idiot?"'

'These complete nonentity people made *TOTP* bland and uninteresting. They weren't any good, you didn't care about them and they seemed utterly fake.'

'They shouldn't even have been on TV, let alone hosting the world's best music show,' agrees Glenn Gregory. 'I just thought, "Andi Peters, why are you here?"'

'There was something nicely eccentric about Jimmy Savile introducing bands that were young enough to be his grandchildren,' notes Richard Fairbrass. 'It was part of *TOTP*'s charm. It got lost when they tried to make it cool.'

In 1991, *TOTP* revamped again. Out went the kiddie show hosts and in came a job lot of identikit presenters whose

**Come fly with me:
Anthea Turner.**

anodyne eyes shone with bland ambition. Just who, exactly, *were* Adrian Rose, Claudia Simon, Femi Oke, Mark Franklin, 'Dutch model' Bear van Beers and Tony 'Laters!' Dortie?

These were dark, dark days on *TOTP* but Mike Read is still able to pinpoint the nadir.

'A window-cleaner hosted one show,' he says. 'He won a competition to host *TOTP*. I asked the producers why, and they said, "It's only presenting."

'I said, "Oh, why not have window-cleaners directing the show and working the cameras, then?" They told me not to be silly. Which was kind of my point.'

Mark Goodier contemplates co-hosting with Andi Peters.

House Of No Fun

Britain's second Summer of Love in 1988 yielded acid house, the most exhilarating youth and music movement since punk.

Heard at ear-perforating volumes at clubs or parties, in an altered state, techno sounded fantastic: a hypnotic, life-altering trip travelled at a pitch of emotional euphoria.

Sadly, watched on *TOTP*, turned down low and sand-wiched between Deacon Blue and Johnny Hates Jazz, the same artists both looked and sounded absolutely terrible.

TOTP had got the point of glam rock and complemented it. It came to an arrangement with punk and gained from its visceral rage. With acid house, it didn't have a clue – and the problems began with Black Box.

In 1989 the Italian dance producers hit No. 1 with 'Ride On Time'. The song was based on a vocal sample of soul star Loleatta Holloway, who went to the papers complaining that she had not given permission.

When Black Box played *TOTP*, viewers thus knew that front woman Katrin was miming to what was somebody else's vocal entirely. The resultant ridicule stung *TOTP* into insisting that all acts must henceforth play live.

They could not have made a worse move.

DJ Sean Rowley now runs retro-kitsch club and record label Guilty Pleasures, but spent the acid house years as

Black Box's Katrin gives the performance of somebody else's life.

Orbital: 'It's not very visual, is it?'

Orbital's plugger. It was not an easy job.

'*TOTP* was born in the 1960s and still had a format that belonged in the 1950s,' he recalls. 'Its old luvvie producers were a lot happier working on *Wogan* and just couldn't get their heads around dance music.

'They said Orbital would have to play live and I said, "They can't, they're not musicians." They said, "How do they make music, then?" I said, "They put samples together of other bits of music." They said, "That's not music!"

'I tried to explain: "Look, they fire off sequencers attached to keyboards …" and they said, "Ah, keyboards! That's OK!" Then I showed them a stage plan of how Orbital set up and it was just two keyboards. They said, "It's not very visual, is it?"'

They had a point. Anonymous alchemists twiddling Roland synthesizers in their bedrooms, the makers of acid house were producers, not pop stars.

N-Joi, Technotronic, Slipstreem, Bassheads and The Grid sounded tremendous in clubs. Live, as *Melody Maker* observed, it was 'like watching spot-welding'.

'*TOTP* would zoom the cameras about to try to liven things up,' remembers William Orbit of Bassomatic. 'Two

> ## 'Two guys standing behind keyboards do not make great TV.'
>
> ### William Orbit, Bassomatic

guys standing behind keyboards do not make great TV.'

Realising this, K-Klass, Bomb The Bass and Beatmasters drafted in sultry divas to provide visual focus. Yazz sang with Coldcut; Cathy Dennis helped out D-Mob. The live vocal thing, though, remained a problem.

Urban Hype nearly gave themselves hernias singing kids' TV samples on 'A Trip To *Trumpton*' while Capella's Kelly Overett struggled with 1994's 'Move On Baby'.

'We were on the same show and *TOTP* made her sing live a looped, layered sample with no pauses for breath,' recalls Bob Stanley. 'It was physically impossible.'

The sense of a show at odds with the music it played only grew when 'Woo!' Gary Davies, asked to introduce 808 State, misread the autocue and instead welcomed Bob State.

The Orb, finally, showed the absurdity of the whole charade with a magnificently subversive 1992 performance. Asked to play 'The Blue Room', Alex Paterson and Thrash instead sat and played chess as the tune's video ran behind them.

'Thrash pissed me off, though,' Paterson later explained. 'I was trying to play properly, but he started cheating and taking random pieces off.'

Britpop Meets The Queen Vic

By 1993, the Top 40 was doing *TOTP* few favours. Plaid-clad **US** grunge rock bands, who normally were not around to plug their hits, vied with faceless, acid-house-inspired dance acts. With ratings plummeting, the BBC gave serious thought to moving *TOTP* to BBC2 – or even axing it completely.

TOTP, which was now filmed at the BBC's Elstree Studios, needed a shot in the arm. It got one.

'Suddenly, the indie charts became the real charts,' Jarvis Cocker of Pulp remembered. 'It was just this really exciting time.'

The catalyst for the Britpop explosion was Blur's unhappy US tour of 1992. The jaunt crystallised Damon Albarn's dislike of the musical dominance of the Nirvana-led Seattle rock scene and the Americanisation of British culture and he returned with a provocative manifesto: 'I'm getting rid of grunge'.

Blur's subsequent *Modern Life Is Rubbish* album opened the floodgates for artists such as Suede and Pulp who similarly celebrated the marvels and mundanities of everyday British life. Yet other factors also facilitated *TOTP*'s resurgence.

The cull of Radio 1's Smashie and Nicey DJs had ushered in hip young gunslingers such as Chris Evans with more contemporary playlists, while *TOTP* had a fresh producer in Radio 1 tyro Ric Blaxill.

'When I took over at *TOTP*, the show was very dance-based,' he recalls. 'I figured there was a wealth of talent and artists around the Top 40 who would broaden the music and characters and entertainment.'

Blur and Suede led the way and many followed. Pulp dramatically ended ten years in the indie wilderness and shot to mainstream fame, while Elastica, Sleeper, The Verve and the Boo Radleys also tumbled onto *TOTP*.

'Elastica were on *TOTP* with The Cranberries doing "Linger", which had this chorus of "*Did you have to let it linger?*"' remembers Phill Savidge, a former press agent for both bands.

'Elastica spent the whole show hanging around outside The Cranberries' dressing room, shouting, "*Did you have to use two fingers?*"'

Some survivors of the late 1980s indie-dance movement also benefited from Britpop. The poetic, giddy James enjoyed a second wind, while Inspiral Carpets escorted a post-punk icon onto *TOTP* – with mixed results.

'We did the "I Want You" single with Mark E Smith from The Fall and went to *TOTP* with him,' recalls Clint Boon. 'He was a whirlwind of chaos.

'Smithy made the receptionist in our hotel cry, then as soon as we got to *TOTP* he went to the canteen and upset Gillian Taylforth off *EastEnders*.

> ## 'Suddenly, the indie charts became the real charts. It was just this really exciting time.'
>
> **Jarvis Cocker**

Suede were one of the first Britpop bands to play *TOTP*.

He was just so cantankerous.

'At rehearsal he was winding up all the cameramen, telling them, "You should have tried harder in school!" We were all pissed and Mark and I ended up having a weird slapping fight and being pulled apart by the band.'

Yet these later arrivals were all dwarfed by the emergence on *TOTP* of the Manchester band who were to help define the decade: Oasis.

Noel Gallagher's personal *TOTP* epiphany had come while watching The Smiths perform 'This Charming Man' in 1983. 'From that moment on,' he confessed, simply, 'I

wanted to *be* Johnny Marr.'

Oasis's *TOTP* debut was 'Shakermaker' in 1994 and Liam Gallagher made his entrance in trademark style.

'Bruno Brookes was introducing us and in rehearsal he said something about, "Now we have a top indie band",' Noel recalled.

'Liam went running over and said, "We're not a fucking indie band, we're a rock 'n' roll band!" So on the show itself, Bruno Brookes said, "They're not an indie band, they're a rock 'n' roll band."'

Noel even believes that the famous antipathy between Oasis and Blur may have had its roots in an innocuous backstage encounter.

'We walked past the make-up room,' he explained. 'We never wear make-up on telly but Blur were all in there and Liam, diplomat that he is, put his head round the door and said, "You look fucking gorgeous." We baited them all day: "I think your mascara is running there, Damon."'

The Oasis/Blur rivalry was in full swing when Albarn guest-hosted *TOTP* in December 1994 and was forced to introduce Oasis singing 'Whatever'.

'Damon was very gracious about it,' says Blaxill. 'Oasis were following Take That, so he decided to say, "And now, here's another five talented blokes from Manchester."

'Every time he said it, Oasis were doing obscene hand signals behind his back. We had to re-take it about five times and even then a rude gesture went out.'

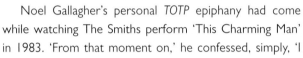

Liam's *Banana Splits* impersonation captivated a nation.

Yet the flashpoint of the struggle between the two Britpop titans came in August 1995, when they went head-to-head with simultaneous single releases: Oasis's 'Roll With It' and Blur's 'Country House'.

After Blur pipped Oasis to No. 1, bassist Alex James sportingly (or provocatively?) wore an Oasis t-shirt at the show's end. Oasis, reliably, were far less gracious.

'I mimed Liam's singing part and he tried to mime playing my guitar,' Noel said. 'If I'd known he was going to do it so badly, I wouldn't have bothered.'

Despite Blur's triumph, Oasis's less arty, more proletarian anthems were to dominate UK music and *TOTP* in the mid-1990s, when Manic Street Preachers, Echobelly, Catatonia and the luscious All Saints were also regular Elstree visitors.

The chemically-inclined rock veterans Primal Scream lucked onto the Britpop bandwagon but gave Blaxill a major headache.

'They had a gig in Dublin the night before and then were supposed to fly back to do "(I'm Gonna) Cry Myself Blind" on *TOTP*,' he recalls.

'The next thing I knew, I got a call on the day of the show saying they weren't coming as they would have to fly into Luton Airport and it wasn't rock 'n' roll enough.'

The Monkees-like Supergrass were scarcely out of school when they became *TOTP* regulars, but that didn't

'I got a call saying Primal Scream weren't coming as they would have to fly into Luton Airport and it wasn't rock 'n roll enough.'

Ric Blaxill, *TOTP* producer

Valley high: Manic Street Preachers.

Spice Girls sing as the *TOTP* crew hose themselves down.

stop them entering into the party spirit.

'We'd spend all day at *TOTP* with our record company giving us drinks and other stuff,' says the drummer Danny Goffey. 'We'd be bleary-eyed and chewing our heads off.'

A *TOTP* acolyte since the age of five, Bluetones singer Mark Morriss had a Damascene conversion on his first visit to the show.

'We were on the road so we arrived at 10 in the morning feeling naff and tired but still very excited about doing *TOTP*,' he remembers.

'We were on with Radiohead and I was croaking around the studio with a cup of tea in my hand at their rehearsal

Heaven tumbling out of Thom Yorke's gob

when Thom Yorke opened his mouth and Heaven came out.

'It was incredible. I wasn't even a big Radiohead fan at the time but it's stayed with me ever since. I thought, "This isn't a game – this guy is an artist."'

Having been fixtures on early 1990s *TOTP*, Take That's impact was arguably exceeded by that of the solo Robbie Williams at the end of the decade. The Spice Girls also descended on Elstree and made an impact both on the screen and off it.

'They used to flirt with everyone,' one *TOTP* crew member later told Jeff Simpson

in his book *Top of the Pops 1964–2002*. 'All of the guys definitely thought they were up for a shag with one of them.'

He was the future once, but Andy McCluskey, the OMD singer who had despised being introduced by 'sad old fuckers' Jimmy Savile and DLT, got his karmic comeuppance.

'In the 1980s the bands thought they were cool and the presenters were cheesy but in

> **'You would go to the canteen and see Tori Amos having a cup of tea and Dot Cotton at the next table.'**
>
> **Alex James, Blur**

the 1990s the boot was on the other foot for us,' he admits. 'Radio 1 had changed its style of DJ and a synth band from the 1980s was considered old hat.

'I remember going into the make-up room and Jo Whiley completely blanking me. Now the DJs were too cool for the band.'

TOTP's 1990s Elstree location might have lacked the

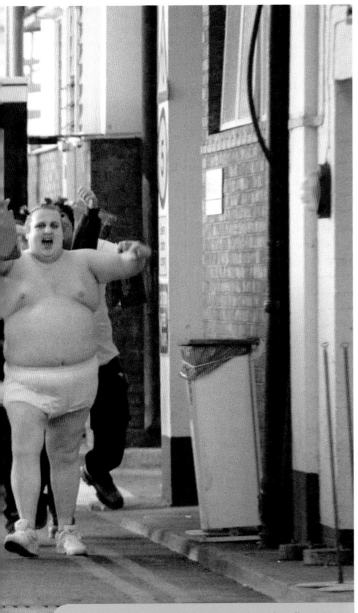

Fat Les celebrate the Queen Vic getting a late licence.

and the café,' boasted John Moore of Black Box Recorder. 'Then we tried to go upstairs in the Fowlers' living-room, the whole house swayed and we were shooed away by a one-legged security guard.'

'We had a wander around the square and had a joint on Arthur Fowler's bench,' says the Bluetones' Morriss, but one *TOTP* old-timer had a less chilled experience.

'I went onto the *EastEnders* set,' recalls Francis Rossi. 'Some bloke in his twenties said, "You can't come in here, son!" and ushered me out. I was 45 years old at the time.'

'We were good friends with Ian Reddington, who played Tricky Dicky,' says Glenn Gregory of Heaven 17. 'He would sneak in to *TOTP* and be overawed by that, while we were going, "Wow! It's the Queen Vic!"'

Fran Healy 'knew Travis had really made it' when the band were recognised by the soap's cast in the Elstree canteen, while indie veterans The Wedding Present left a tiny mark on Walford.

'After we'd recorded *TOTP*, we took a spin around Albert Square in our tour van,' admits David Gedge. 'The streets were so narrow that we kept hitting the kerbs. Two of the band added their names to the graffiti on the café door.'

When Fat Les performed the 1998 World Cup anthem 'Vindaloo', a 75-strong chanting mob including Keith Allen, Matt Lucas, David Walliams and Paul Kaye yomped from Albert Square to a *TOTP* stage, pausing in rehearsal to abuse the passing Spice Girls: '*Where the fuck are you from? We're from En-ger-land!*'

Yet when the fictional borough of Walford developed urban sprawl, *TOTP* was given its own marching orders.

'We got kicked out of Elstree to give *EastEnders* more room,' says Jeff Simpson, who was on *TOTP*'s production team. 'The first that we knew about it was when one of their location managers turned up and started measuring our set.

'We asked him what he was doing, and he said, "This is going to be Pat Butcher's kitchen."'

**Tricky Dicky: 'Keep it down or
I'll send the Mitchells round!'**

glamour and tradition of Television Centre, but it had one major plus point for visiting British artists: it also housed the set of *EastEnders*. Inevitably, a parade of bands set off on a mission to infiltrate Albert Square.

'You would go to the canteen and see Tori Amos having a cup of tea and Dot Cotton at the next table,' remembered Alex James of Blur. 'At first you could get into Albert Square but then they put gates around it.'

'There was a bad girl character called Mandy in *East-Enders* and we saw her playing pool in the canteen with East 17,' says St Etienne's Bob Stanley. 'That seemed about right.'

'We snuck into the Queen Vic, Pauline's laundrette

Which Camera Am I On?

The odds are long that you will turn on your TV set to find Johnny Vegas reading the BBC *Ten O'Clock News*. Nor has Su Pollard been asked to present *Panorama*, or Nadia Almada from *Big Brother 6* deputed to host *Match of the Day*.

With blithe disregard for such conventions, *TOTP* frequently invited awestruck guests from all walks of life to present its weekly pop party. The results can safely be described as mixed.

Davy Jones from the Monkees hosted *TOTP* in 1968 while the early 1980s saw some odd couplings of stars and DJs: Elton John with Peter Powell, Cliff Richard with Steve Wright and the tonsorially troubling duo of Kevin Keegan and Dave Lee Travis.

The pairing of Tommy Vance and The Who singer Roger Daltrey in August 1980 resulted in the following exchange:

Vance: 'Do you like disco, Roger?'

Daltrey: 'No, I hate it!'

Vance: 'Oh, that's a shame, because here's the Village People and "Can't Stop The Music"!'

'Backs against the wall!' advised a smirking Daltrey as the camera panned to the gyrating New Yorkers. These were truly less enlightened times.

Yet the zenith of the guest presenter fad came in the Britpop period, when producer Ric Blaxill introduced a would-be iconic 'golden mic' and plonked a

Ric Blaxill: 'We had artists, comedians, sports personalities, the lot.'

> ## 'I thought INXS was a stupid name so I called them Inks.'
>
> ### Jarvis Cocker

succession of startled-looking major and minor pop culture figures in front of the *TOTP* cameras.

'We had artists, comedians, sports personalities, the lot,' muses Blaxill. 'I just figured if you turned on and saw someone you didn't expect, you might stick with it a bit longer.'

Britpop was thus marked by a series of presenters that suggested producers had stuck a pin into a celeb directory. Kylie, Robbie and Neneh Cherry kind of made sense as *TOTP* hosts: Angus Deayton, Frankie Dettori and Julia Carling arguably less so.

'Meat Loaf was hosting *TOTP* and I gave him a script that started, "Intro: Terrorvision",' remembers Blaxill.

'He said, "This is *TOTP*" then just screamed: "AAARGH!" All the kids went quiet so I went down and said, "Meat, that's effective, but what are you doing?"

'He told me, "I'm following your concept, man – Terrorvision!" I said, "They're a band," and he said, "Oh, I thought you wanted me to scare the hell out of the audience."'

Jarvis Cocker happily proved more finely tuned to the nuances of the mid-1990s music scene. Charged with introducing boy band Let Loose, he sniffed like a man coming across a noxious smell and asked, 'Who's let loose? Oh, it's them!'

'I thought INXS was a stupid name, so I called them Inks,' he recalled. 'They kept messing up, then Michael Hutchence said, "Is there any chance the presenter could get our name right?"'

Ant and Dec, then trading as PJ and Duncan, upset the talent when they

Julia Carling tries to remember the last pop record she bought.

defined Courtney Love as 'Kurt Cobain's widow', which caused the tired and emotional Love to stop her rehearsal to harangue them from the stage.

At Britpop's apex in August 1995, Blur and Oasis staged the great 'Country House' v 'Roll With It' face-off. It's debatable whether the high drama was increased by the result being announced by Dale Winton.

'At the time, I was hosting *Supermarket Sweep* and *Pets Win Prizes*,' he reflected. 'I loved doing *TOTP*, but in some ways it would have made as much sense to invite Thora Hird.'

'East 17 were presenting *TOTP* the first time we were on,' remembers the Bluetones singer Mark Morriss. 'Tony Mortimer called us the Blue Notes.'

The supposedly comic duos Punt and Dennis and Hale and Pace made their own families laugh – maybe – but Paul Kaye, a.k.a. geek-guerrilla reporter Dennis Pennis, hit home harder.

'He said Chris de Burgh looked like a mole and said about Skunk Anansie: "They're well named because they're black, white and their music really stinks,"' says Blaxill. 'Luckily it was so loud in the studio, they couldn't hear him.'

Yet even Pennis's subversive efforts could not compete with the unintentional comic genius of world middleweight boxing champion Chris Eubank.

'I phoned Eubank up and said, "We're using presenters who are pop stars, actors or sports personalities and have charisma and attitude,"' recalls Blaxill. 'He said, "You're so lucky, because I'm all of those."'

Arriving hours late, Eubank chose to do the dress rehearsal in his underpants. It was not his garb but his famous lisp that was his undoing when he had to tell the nation that this particular week No. 6 was the sensational 'Cecilia' by Suggs: 'It was hard to sing with a straight face,' the Madness thinger, er, singer was to confess.

'Chris also had to introduce Sleeper's "Sale Of The Century",' remembers Blaxill. 'He asked me if we were taking the piss, but it was just the way it worked out.'

The ludicrously over-excitable Arsenal and England striker Ian Wright dyed his hair bright yellow in honour of hosting *TOTP*, a course of action that Gary Olsen, Harry Hill and Ardal O'Hanlon failed to follow.

'Julian Cope presented one show and brought all these friends like Swampy, who were protesting against the

Chris Eubank got some thtick after hosting *TOTP*.

PJ and Duncan rumbled with Courtney Love.

Nevertheless, *TOTP* occasionally returned to celebrity presenters in its twilight years, when frantic format rethinks seemed a weekly blight.

The veteran crooner Tony Christie revisited the show in 2005 to perform his No. 1 '(Is This The Way To) Amarillo' and was surprised to be introduced by *Top Gear*'s bumptious Jeremy Clarkson.

'He made some sarcastic comment about my Cuban heels,' Christie recalls. 'I didn't see the need for that.'

'I turned on *TOTP* and there was Jeremy Clarkson,' marvels Tony Blackburn. 'He was very funny but absolutely wrong for the programme.

'I remember there was an American rap bloke on. When

Dennis Pennis menaced *TOTP* egos.

Newbury by-pass,' remembers Blaxill.

'They had loads of anti-government messages and I got in a lot of trouble over it, but I figured it didn't hurt the programme at all.'

Blaxill's anything-goes regime ended in 1997 with guest spots by Rhona Cameron, Phil Daniels, Dannii Minogue and the Spice Girls. But his flinging open the *TOTP* doors to non-DJs had not gone down well with some people.

DJs, for example.

'*TOTP* wasn't broke so there was no need to fix it,' notes Jimmy Savile. 'Did it work? No, because the viewing figures went down.'

Mike Read is even more scathing about the innovation: 'That was the start of the slippery slope for *TOTP*. They felt that anyone could present, which isn't true. Some of the guest hosts just stood there like deer in headlights.'

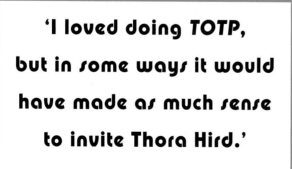

'I loved doing *TOTP*, but in some ways it would have made as much sense to invite Thora Hird.'

Dale Winton

he had finished, Clarkson said, "God, that was awful!"'

Nearing its last, *TOTP* even arranged a return presenting stint for one of the unquestioned icons of its 1970s pomp – the tartan-suited Noddy Holder.

'It was a very different show from when Slade were always on, but in some ways it was just the same,' reflects the unflappable Noddy.

'I did notice that one of the floor managers had also been there on our debut in 1970.'

> **'There was an American rap bloke on. When he had finished, Clarkson said, "God, that was awful!"'**
>
> **Tony Blackburn**

Down with the kid: Jeremy Clarkson with Fearne Cotton.

One For Sorrow

In 1964, US politician Dick Tuck ran as a Democrat candidate for California's State Senate. Having been defeated, he delivered a famously pithy concession address: 'The people have spoken … the bastards.'

TOTP's rigid format of each show climaxing with that week's No. 1 frequently had viewers internally echoing Tuck's aphorism, as seemingly mediocre tracks clung on to the Thursday evening 7.55pm slot for what seemed like forever.

The 1960s may have been swinging but that didn't stop Ken Dodd, Jim Reeves, Tom Jones, Englebert Humperdinck and *Opportunity Knocks* winner Mary Hopkin having five-week runs at No. 1 and *TOTP* ending the decade with Rolf Harris's 'Two Little Boys' on top for six weeks.

Hipsters similarly despaired in 1971 when Dawn's five-week tenure at No. 1 with 'Tie A Yellow Ribbon (Round The Ole Oak Tree)' gave way to an identical period of domination for Middle Of The Road's 'Chirpy Chirpy Cheep Cheep'.

'I was 13 in 1975 and in a band playing two-minute punk-type songs and I hated it when *TOTP* ended with "Bohemian Rhapsody" for nine weeks,' sighs Craig Reid of the Proclaimers. 'It got on my bloody wick.'

As 1977 ended, a sense of existential despair descended upon pockets of the nation every Thursday night at 7.55 as Wings' 'Mull Of Kintyre' refused

Luckily, Middle of the Road kept the receipts from the boutique.

to budge from the top spot for nine weeks.

Grease ruled Britain the following year, with John Travolta and Olivia Newton-John (or Neutron-Bomb, as DLT wittily had it) spending nine weeks at No. 1 with 'You're The One That I Want' followed by seven weeks at the top spot for 'Summer Nights'.

When the Boomtown Rats' 'Rat Trap' finally knocked the latter off the top, Bob Geldof showily ripped up a photo of Travolta and Newton-John on *TOTP*.

The 1980s provided arguably the worst atrocity exhibition of leaden No. 1s draping themselves over *TOTP*'s

A nation implored Bryan Adams to Friar Tuck off.

climax like particularly smothering wet blankets.

Like lumbering beasts on Noah's Ark, they came in pairs. Billy Joel's 'Uptown Girl' spent five weeks on top in November 1983 before the Flying Pickets' 'Only You' relieved it and did exactly the same thing.

The following year, Lionel Richie's seemingly interminable 'Hello' and Stevie Wonder's 'I Just Called To Say I Love You' ruled the roost for six weeks each, while in 1985 *TOTP* was poleaxed by Paul Hard-castle's '19' and Jennifer Rush's shoulder-heaving bombast-ballad 'The Power of Love'.

Yet these were mere trifles next to '(Everything I Do) I Do It For You', Bryan Adams' theme to Kevin Costner's movie *Robin, Prince of Thieves*, which went to No. 1 on July 13, 1991 and stayed there for 16 weeks.

> ### 'What amazed me is how Bryan Adams was No.1 forever and yet nobody ever admitted to buying it.'
>
> **Richard Fairbrass, Right Said Fred**

chagrin of the Troggs singer.

'I still can't believe Wet Wet Wet did that,' sighs Presley. 'I wanted to beat that Robin 'ood song and have the most weeks at No. 1 and in one more week we'd have done it. I were right miffed.'

Such was the mood of national ennui at the Wets' ubiquity during the summer of '94 that one up-and-coming star got positively militant.

'Pulp were doing "Babies" on *TOTP*,' explained Jarvis Cocker. 'Halfway through the song, I opened up my jacket to show a sign that said "I HATE WET WET WET".

'Of course, it made no difference at all, and it went on to be the biggest-selling record of the year.'

The people have spoken… the bastards.

'What amazed me,' mulls Richard Fairbrass, 'is how Bryan Adams was No. 1 forever and yet nobody ever admitted to buying it.'

Costner was an accessory to a further musical crime in December 1992, when Whitney Houston's 'I Will Always Love You' theme from *The Bodyguard* annexed the end of *TOTP* until the following February.

Adams' record was threat-ened only once. On June 4, 1994, Wet Wet Wet's 'Love Is All Around', the theme to Hugh Grant's gosh-golly *Four Weddings And A Funeral*, written by Reg Presley, debuted at No. 1.

Wet Wet Wet closed *TOTP* all that summer and autumn leaves were falling from the trees when the band, bored with the song, withdrew it from sale in October… to the huge

Did You See That?

The most inspirational pop music transforms and elevates its surroundings, introducing a flash of mercurial brilliance into the dreariness of the everyday. In its gawky, cack-handed way, *TOTP* delivered many such moments that changed the way people viewed the world.

It could be profound, could be preposterous, but every now and then *TOTP* produced a seminal image that scarred into the memory banks like battery acid.

'I'll never forget The Who's wild antics and Pete Townshend's helicopter whirls on guitar,' says Tony Christie. 'I just thought, "My God! They should be in cages!"'

'They were on the next stage to me when Pete Townshend broke his guitar and kicked over all the amps,' concurs Lynsey de Paul. 'I was cowering from the flying debris.'

Years before T Rex boogied through 'Metal Guru' or Bowie camped up 'Starman', cult loon the Crazy World of Arthur Brown lit up *TOTP* by setting fire to a colander full of paper strapped to his head for his No. 1 in 1968, 'Fire'.

Likewise, in the days when *Monty Python* ruled the comedic roost, the Bonzo Dog Doo Dah Band pleased self-professed nutters by performing 'I'm The Urban Spaceman' dressed as ballerinas from the waist down and male dancers from the waist up.

Rather more significantly,

> ## 'I'll never forget The Who's wild antics. I just thought, "My God! They should be in cages!"'
>
> **Tony Christie**

Beatles fans were agog in February 1970 when, with the Fab Four still not officially dead, John Lennon checked in to *TOTP* to play 'Instant Karma'.

Yoko Ono, at that point probably the most hated woman in Britain, did little to improve her PR image by holding up a series of signs reading 'Peace' and 'Love' while blindfolded by a sanitary towel.

This had an inexplicable effect on The Members singer Nick Tesco, who was then a pupil at boarding school: 'It finished and we all went fucking bananas and trashed a whole floor of the school,' he remembers. 'I later got expelled.'

The same month saw a less seismic but equally bizarre *TOTP* in which session musician Tony Burrows sang the lead vocal on three consecutive studio hits: Brotherhood of Man's 'United We Stand', 'My Baby Loves Lovin'' by White Plains and Edison Lighthouse's 'Love Grows (Where My Rosemary Goes)'.

'I had to keep changing clothes on the side of the stage,' the admirably prolific Burrows later recalled, but the incident resulted in him receiving an unofficial two-year ban from the BBC: 'They told me it just didn't look right.'

Sometimes *TOTP* hit home through sheer exuberance. One heavy-drinking day in 1971 saw Rod Stewart and his band play football against Slade in the BBC's corridors, then try to burst in on Pan's People while they were changing.

Yoko Ono finds a novel use for a Bodyform Super.

The Crazy World of Arthur Brown: Health and Safety is for squares.

Taking to the stage to perform 'Maggie May', Stewart insisted that John Peel should mime playing the mandolin and continued to kick footballs round the studio; Ronnie Wood jumped off the stage well before the song had ended.

'That was my favourite *TOTP* performance of all time,' Noel Gallagher later enthused. 'I particularly loved Rod's yellow tartan trousers.'

Glam-rock era *TOTP* was never far from its next jaw-dropping surprise and The Osmonds' white-suited, leg-cocking dance that accompanied their No. 2 'Crazy Horses' in 1974 was certainly among them.

'My brother Jay invented that,' muses Donny. 'He knew some Mormon missionary who came back from Samoa and showed us how the people there danced and then Jay threw in this random arm movement. Genius, huh?'

'I remember seeing the piano player from Mud eating some flowers that were on top of his piano,' says Johnny Sharp, a wide-eyed 1970s pop fan who now writes for the *Guardian*. 'I was about five and it seemed like the most insane thing that anyone had ever done.

'Also, my dad and I watched Freddie Mercury playing piano and crossing one hand over the other on "Bohemian Rhapsody". He seemed like a circus magician. My dad said that he was "talented but a bit effeminate".'

'I think I had my first wet dream to Pan's People,' mulls Keith Mullen of The Farm, and Flick Colby's sexed-up shock troupe gave *TOTP* viewers some unforgettable moments.

'They danced to Smokey Robinson's "Tears of a Clown", which naturally involved a clown and a bucket of water,' recalls Sean Rowley of Guilty Pleasures.

'A lot of people say that when they saw Bowie hugging Mick Ronson, they knew that they were gay. Well, when I saw one of Pan's People, up a stepladder, pouring water over another of Pan's People, I knew that I was straight.'

Def Leppard singer Joe Elliott has talked in awed tones of watching Elvis Costello, in a flying harness, bouncing around the *TOTP* studio for 'I Can't Stand Up For Falling Down'.

All together now: 'Nwaah! Nwaah!'

Kate Bush: the Brontës had never seemed so sexy.

Costello's fellow new wavers John Otway and Wild Willy Barrett jumped out of view in a rather different way.

'We'd just been on the *Old Grey Whistle Test* doing "Really Free",' Otway recalled. 'I'd tried to leap on the amplifier and landed on my bollocks and that stunt had taken the song into the charts.

'We tried to repeat the trick on *TOTP* and insisted on doing it live, just for good measure. To be honest, it was absolute chaos.'

On a rather more ethereal level, Kate Bush seared into the national conscious-ness when she made her *TOTP* debut in 1978, sitting at a grand piano like a sexy wraith as she crooned the spectral dream-pop of 'Wuthering Heights' like no performer who had come before.

Pop is an innately subjective pleasure and Squeeze singer Glenn Tilbrook felt a tran-scendent thrill in 1979 where others might have found only throwaway synth-pop.

'We were on the same show as M doing "Pop Music" and hearing it just gave me a huge buzz,' he recalls. 'It seemed such a special record, so apart from everything else.'

Naturally, some of *TOTP*'s most famous episodes were elevated to the pantheon by acts of slapstick subversion rather than musical magnifi-cence.

In 1982, Dexy's Midnight Runners gambolled through 'Jackie Wilson Said' in front of a backdrop not of the soul legend, but of the 16-stone Scottish darts player Jocky Wilson.

'For a laugh, we told the producer to put a picture of Jocky Wilson behind us,' Dexy's singer Kevin Rowland later explained. 'He said, "But Kevin, people will think we've made a mistake." I told him only an idiot would think that.

'The next morning on Radio 1, Mike Read said, "Honestly, *TOTP*. How could they mix up one of the great soul singers with a Scottish darts player?"'

'For a laugh, we told the producer to put a picture of Jocky Wilson behind us.'

Kevin Rowland, Dexy's Midnight Runners

Even the dreariest *TOTP* artists could surprise with a flash of wit. Shortly after his wife had run off with the man who decorated their house, Phil Collins crooned 'In The Air Tonight' with a pot of paint and a brush on top of his grand piano.

Steeped in *TOTP* history and lore, The Smiths invariably went the extra mile to ensure that their string of eagerly-received mid-1980s appearances were out of the ordinary.

Suavely introverted in NHS spectacles and hearing aid and waving gladioli at the throng, Morrissey seemed like an emissary from an edgier, more curious world. For 'The Boy With The Thorn In His Side', he etched the word 'Bad' on his neck.

'I was transfixed when they played "William, It Was Really Nothing" and Morrissey ripped his shirt open and had "Marry Me" written on his chest in lipstick,' says Bob Stanley of St Etienne. 'That was pretty spectacular.'

'Madness were doing "Night Boat To Cairo" in shorts and pith helmets and Morrissey was on the next stage doing "Heaven Knows I'm Miserable Now",' recalled Suggs. 'I suddenly thought, "Oh my goodness, what am I doing wearing shorts and a pith helmet?"'

'*TOTP* was a fantastic forum for Morrissey and a great platform for his ideas,' agrees Johnny Marr. 'They quite rightly became talking points in our band's history.'

Light years away from the Smiths' erudite ethos, Madonna and Cyndi Lauper excited attention when they made their *TOTP* debuts on the same show in 1984. Madonna skipped and bopped through 'Holiday' while Lauper ran around the studio and up to the gantry for 'Girls Just Wanna Have Fun'.

Madonna upped the ante when she returned later in the year for 'Like A Virgin' and writhed around the floor in a studded leather jacket, fishnets, fluorescent green leg-warmers and a long pink wig – a performance that overnight won her legions of teenage girl fans.

TOTP host Steve Wright was less impressed. 'Madonna kept doing take after take and I wanted to get home because my mum was making a shepherd's pie,' he recalled.

'I went over to Madonna and said, "Look, love, my mum's doing me a shepherd's pie, could you please hurry up?" She looked at me as if I was insane and has never spoken to me since.'

The KLF always created a *TOTP* stir. They drafted in Gary Glitter before his fall from grace and a homemade Dalek for 'Doctorin' The Tardis' (performed under the alias of the Timelords), and thereafter favoured monks' habits with rhino horns protruding from their foreheads.

Indie insurrectionists Manic Street Preachers took a leaf from Morrissey's book on their debut appearance, playing 'You Love Us', when bassist Nicky Wire scrawled the phrase on his chest in lipstick.

Nevertheless, it could have been far more spectacular: Wire had earnestly promised the music press that, if his band

ever got on *TOTP*, he would set fire to himself on the show.

TOTP and grunge were no more natural bedfellows than had been *TOTP* and punk, which led to Nirvana's sole visit to the show in 1991 being a truly tectonic encounter.

Arriving both mentally and physically out of sorts, Kurt Cobain asked permission to mime 'Smells Like Teen Spirit' but was refused. Exasperated by this reversal, Cobain droned the song in a pitch-black growl and radically rewrote the opening line: '*Load up on drugs, kill your friends*'.

Cobain proceeded to strum his fingers insouciantly inches from his guitar frets while Krist Novoselic brandished his bass over his head like a weapon and Dave Grohl jigged in his seat before demolishing his drum kit, helped by the leaders of a spontaneous stage invasion.

At times, *TOTP* appeared to be its own hermetic universe. Its producers seemed willing to ask artists to do things they would usually cavil at – and more often that not the perplexed performers would toe the line.

'We played some special anniversary *TOTP* show and the producers wanted to go out with "Rockin' All Over The World",' remembers Francis Rossi.

'They made all the other acts who had been on the show before us come and stand in front of us and dance while we were playing, including the Beach Boys. The bloody Beach Boys! Dancing to Status Quo!

'We didn't half take the piss out of them about that one later.'

> **'I went over to Madonna and said, "Look, love, my mum's doing me a shepherd's pie, could you please hurry up?" She looked at me as if I was insane and has never spoken to me since.'**
>
> **Steve Wright**

Madonna: like no virgin you'd ever seen before.

Nirvana made sure their *TOTP* visit was a one-off.

Why Oh Why Oh Why?

Rock 'n' roll is largely about transgression, so it is no surprise that *TOTP* has attracted thousands of viewer complaints over the years: it would not be doing its job had it not. Yet it was often hard to foresee exactly what would get Middle England seething.

'My girlfriend's dad phoned the BBC in a red-faced rage when he saw Larry Blackmon of Cameo's external codpiece,' says one 1980s pop fan. 'He was very proud of that.'

When Marsha Hunt performed 'Walking On Gilded Splinters' in 1969, one of her breasts fell out of her halter-top. However, as Ms Hunt was then starring in the nude musical *Hair*, you could kind of see it coming.

Pregnancy rendered some *TOTP* viewers squeamish. Mary Hopkin in 1976 and Kirsty MacColl a decade later were both asked to wear loose clothes to conceal their expectant state from the nation.

In the Britpop years, the switchboard lit up for the Prodigy's 'Firestarter' video and also when the show tried to create 'an image of hell' for INXS's 'The Strangest Party'.

'We had gothic performance artists on stilts who were eating fire and juggling,' recalls *TOTP* producer Ric Blaxill. 'I had to go on a BBC complaints show because it frightened small children.'

The *Points of View* malcontents grumbled when Robbie Williams stripped down to his tiger pants on 'Rock DJ' and again when the boy band Phixx performed a bondage-based dance routine. It's unclear if the complaints were about the routine or the very existence of Phixx.

Hip-hop has little truck with social propriety and the BBC had to apologise after both 50 Cent and The Game turned the *TOTP* air blue in 2005. Some easily disgusted souls were on such a hair-trigger that they lodged pre-emptive complaints.

'When Eamon got to No. 1 with 'Fuck It (I Don't Want You Back)', *Daily Mail* readers wrote to me, saying, "How dare you let him say the F-word 33 times on *TOTP*!"' says producer Andi Peters. 'I thought, "Of course I'm not going to."'

Yet it was the Manic Street Preachers who proved *TOTP*'s deadliest agents provocateurs.

> '**I let fly with a string of expletives and he told me, "You will never work on this show again."**'
>
> **Robert Wyatt**

So here's to you, Mrs Robinson.

In 1994, they played 'Faster' in combat gear and balaclavas. Assuming it was in homage to IRA terrorists, more than 25,000 people phoned in.

'We thought it would get a reaction but we were parodying legitimate power, like special forces,' claimed James Dean Bradfield. 'It never even occurred to us that people would see it as an Irish paramilitary symbol.'

Now and then, *TOTP* saw viewer trouble coming and tried to head it off at the pass. When The Cure played 'Lullaby' in 1989, the director banned close-up shots of erratically made-up singer Robert Smith, lest his fizogg scare the horses.

In 2004, Pete Doherty and Wolfman reached No. 2 with 'For Lovers' but *TOTP* barred the unkempt Wolfman. Which begs the question of how bad you need to look before Pete Doherty is chosen over you as the acceptable face of your band.

And, just occasionally, *TOTP* got it horribly, grotesquely wrong. In 1974, wheelchair-bound singer Robert Wyatt visited the show to plug his cover of the Monkees' 'I'm A Believer'.

'The producer asked me to get out of my wheelchair and sit in a raffia chair,' Wyatt recalls. 'I didn't want to because it looked very unstable. I hadn't long been in a wheelchair and wasn't very confident.

'He said, "You can't sit in that, this is a family show." I let fly with a string of expletives and he told me, "You will never work on this show again!" Which is exactly what happened.

Take that! Robbie unleashes the tiger in his tank.

Pete: 'Look mate, you need to sort yourself out.'

The Show Must Go Off

So, who killed *TOTP*? When the BBC's axe finally fell on the world's longest-running music show and the blame game began, various suspects quickly emerged.

The main culprit was today's multimedia environment of satellite music TV channels, digital downloads and online communities such as MySpace. This multiplicity of options for access to music clearly made the concept of *TOTP* – a weekly, must-see pop show – a quaint anachronism.

A significant number of artists and viewers pointed the finger at Andi Peters, the executive producer who was parachuted in for one last despairing *TOTP* revamp in 2003. Yet the first blow was struck by Vera Duckworth.

In 1996, *TOTP* was moved from the Thursday night slot it had occupied for 32 years to run against ITV's *Coronation Street* on Friday nights. The combination of Weatherfield and Friday being a natural 'night out' inevitably hit viewing figures.

'Moving *TOTP* from Thursday to Friday night changed everything,' noted Pete Waterman, one of the many critics of the switch. 'It just ain't the same.'

'I had problems with that move,' concurred Jarvis Cocker. 'It was stuck in my mind since I could remember – *TOTP* is Thursday.'

Nevertheless, the Britpop bounce initially softened the

> ### 'Moving TOTP from Thursday to Friday night changed everything. It just ain't the same.'
>
> **Pete Waterman**

blow, with Oasis, Spice Girls and Robbie Williams now staples of the show. 'Why am I good for *TOTP*?' said Williams. 'Charisma, good looks, charm, fantastic singing voice and a huge cock.'

In 1997 the new producer, Chris Cowey, a veteran of alternative rock shows like *The Tube* and *The White Room*, instigated a back-to-basics *TOTP* overhaul.

Declaring that '*TOTP* is a great British invention, like football or fish and chips,' Cowey set about reinstating the formula of the show's 1970s halcyon days, including returning to (a remix of) the classic 'Whole Lotta Love' theme tune.

Banishing the intrusive guest presenters ('They just want to promote themselves') Cowey went back to *TOTP*'s original set-up of four presenters in rotation, with the carefully cool (if somewhat bland) Jamie Theakston, Jo Whiley, Zoë Ball and Jayne Middlemiss.

Yet the main problem facing *TOTP* was the devalued currency of the singles chart. With most major releases debuting in the Top 5, and normally at No. 1, Johnnie Stewart's 1964-vintage rules of only playing tracks working their way up the Top 40 no longer made sense. Regretfully, Cowey abandoned them.

'We would be on with loads of shit rave acts,' remembers

Green Day were regulars on a rockier *TOTP*.

DLT would have been proud of the onstage wackiness of namesakes Travis.

Mark Morriss of the Bluetones. 'It would be just a guy and a girl and a dance box and you'd think, "Christ Almighty, how is *this* No. 3?"'

Instead, Cowey shifted the focus to rock and indie. With greater flexibility over who could appear, Stereophonics, Green Day and nu-metallers like Limp Bizkit and Linkin Park became turn-of-the-millennium *TOTP* regulars.

As ever, *TOTP* produced water-cooler moments. Performing 'The Real Slim Shady' live via satellite link in 2000, a narked Eminem unleashed a string of bleeped-out expletives that climaxed with the memorable instruction

'Shut your fucking face, Uncle Europe!'

Scottish band Travis also staged the first *TOTP* food fight since Roy Wood custard-pied Noddy Holder at Christmas 1973.

'Our video for "Sing" had a food fight in it and we decided to rehash it on *TOTP*,' says Fran Healy. 'They gave us *Tiswas*-style custard pies made of shaving foam but I said, "No, it's got to be proper cream cakes."

'Two or three people went and cleared out all the bakers in the local area and I got pasted as I was trying to sing a live vocal. It was absolutely excellent.'

Yet despite its enhanced credibility, Friday night *TOTP* was fighting a King Canute battle against a changing world of wall-to-wall pop TV and diminishing singles sales. Audience figures continued to drop and in 2003 Cowey made way for a new executive producer.

After graduating from children's TV to presenting *TOTP* in the early 1990s, Andi Peters had gone on to host the BBC's Saturday morning show *Live & Kicking* and helped to create Channel 4's T4 programming strand.

Regarded as an expert on youth TV, Peters returned to *TOTP* with a determined agenda.

'I inherited a very guitar- and indie-based show, despite

> ## 'At 7pm on BBC1 on a Friday night, people don't want guitars – they want pop.'
>
> ### Andi Peters

the fact the chart was mostly pop and R&B,' he declares. 'That was wrong, because at 7pm on BBC1 on a Friday night, people don't want guitars – they want pop.'

Feeling that the audience was craving a regular weekly presenter 'that they could get to know,' Peters turned to Tim Kash, an upbeat, unremarkable 21-year-old MTV VJ.

'Tim was young and from an ethnic minority, which *TOTP* had never had before,' he says, somehow overlooking the broadcasting legend that was Tony 'Laters!' Dortie.

'He also brought with him a little bit of credibility because he was from MTV.' To his huge credit, Peters keeps an entirely straight face while making this statement.

So many stylists, yet Pussycat Dolls looked so natural!

Fearne and Reggie: wonder what Fearne's Top 10 Led Zep songs are?

Now reinstated at Television Centre, *TOTP* relaunched with a spectacular stunt. For Blazin' Squad's 'Flip/Reverse', one hundred hooded teenagers performed a choreographed dance routine in the BBC car park.

Despite its ratings slide, *TOTP* was still able to pull in pop's big names. With US R&B and hip-hop dominating the Top 40, the show enjoyed an influx of pop divas.

Janet Jackson insisted that her dressing room be transformed into an Arabian tent, employing a lackey to staple muslin to the walls and – a crucial detail – install a treasure chest.

This demand appeared modest next to Jennifer Lopez, who required ten dressing rooms to house her 60-person entourage. Each room, naturally, had to contain an orchid.

'We tried to give Whitney Houston the best dressing room, which was upstairs, but her management blocked it,' says Jeff Simpson. 'They told us, "Whitney doesn't do stairs."'

'I was on a show with Mariah Carey,' Jarvis Cocker remembered. 'When it was her turn to perform, loads of security guards formed a shape like the prow of a ship around her and walked her to the stage.

'They parted, she sang the song, then they re-formed and walked her back to her room so she didn't have to talk to anybody who had not been screened. It was totally weird.'

Pussycat Dolls' entourage included separate hair gurus, make-up experts and stylists for each Doll: 'I genuinely thought it was the audience arriving,' admits Peters.

> ## 'We tried to give Whitney Houston the best dressing room, but we were told: "Whitney doesn't do stairs."'
>
> **Jeff Simpson**

Keeping it real, R Kelly arrived at the BBC with a mere 43 security guards.

On-screen, *TOTP* did not lack for talking points: Justin Timberlake donning a dolphin costume to perform with acid rockers the Flaming Lips was a genuine coup. The show was also not afraid to resort to a little subterfuge.

'*TOTP* told us they wouldn't let us play because they didn't trust us, but they wanted to do an interview,' says Maggot of Welsh rappers Goldie Lookin' Chain.

'They got three of us to a studio basement in Soho, got the cameras rolling, and said, "We are in Newport, south Wales, with Goldie Lookin' Chain!" We thought, "Eh?"'

Yet bling, novelty turns and sleights of hand were not working. Despite frequent format rethinks, *TOTP*'s audience kept on falling – and the pop world was not impressed.

'We started wondering if we should still do it,' says Danny Goffey of Supergrass, a view shared by Fran Healy: '*TOTP* had been so watered-down, it didn't taste of anything any more. It felt like it was on a life-support machine.'

Having decided Tim Kash 'didn't have enough broadcasting experience', Peters let his contract lapse and, ignoring the lessons of the past, turned to kids' TV for his replacements.

'Fearne Cotton and Reggie Yates had performed well on Children's BBC,' he says. 'They were young, vibrant and aspirational and, when they talked about the artists, people believed them.

'They could introduce the Crazy Frog and make you think, "Hey, it's fun and it's No. 1!"'

Justin Timberlake Flippers, sorry, flips his lid.

Andi Peters had a vision. Unfortunately.

Let us pause for a second, dear reader, while you fully ingest that statement.

Andi Peters had one last masterstroke to pull. In November 2004, two months after Cotton and Yates had joined and with less than three million people still watching, he moved *TOTP* from its Friday night slot to Sunday evenings – on BBC2.

'We moved it to Sunday to follow the new chart on Radio 1,' Peters explains. 'But it was still up against a soap, *Emmerdale*, which was a disaster.

'At that point I left the programme because I was getting so much bad publicity. People were blaming me for *TOTP*'s demise, and I didn't want that.'

And did he still watch the show after quitting the sinking ship? 'No. It wasn't on at a very convenient time for me.'

The programme had been firmly marginalised and there was no way back. On June 20, 2006, with average viewing figures down to 1.5 million, the BBC announced that, after 42 years, *TOTP* was being pulled.

The typical reaction from performers who had graced its stages was a mixture of anger, disappointment – and relief that an ailing institution had finally been put out of its misery.

'I went back a few times in its later years and hardly recognised it from the show that I did in the 1970s,' says

Tony Christie. 'It seemed to have lost its will to live and the presenters were like quiz show hosts.'

'I caught a show towards the end and thought, "What have they done to it? Yuk!"' says 1970s host Emperor Rosko. 'It lacked variety. What else did it lack? Pan's People!'

'It was awful by the end, like watching a goldfish out of its bowl flapping around the floor as it dies,' Andy McCluskey of OMD agrees. 'But I was incredibly sad to see it go.'

Yet Tony Blackburn, one of the superstar DJs of the show's supernova years, was to prove briskly unsentimental about *TOTP*'s death.

'*TOTP* had to come off,' he reflects. 'By the end, I wasn't watching it and my daughter, who was nine years old when it ended, wasn't watching it either. She was watching MTV.

'I sat her down to watch one of the last *TOTP* episodes and see what she thought, and she lost interest after 10 minutes. I thought, "It doesn't appeal to me, it doesn't appeal to her – who *does* it appeal to?"'

Who killed *TOTP*? An uncaring media world watched it perish, Andi Peters' fingerprints were arguably on the smoking gun – but, in truth, it died of old age. Pete Murray, one of its original presenters, discerns no great murder mystery.

'Let's face it, it ran for nearly as long as *The Mousetrap*,' he reckons. 'Maybe that is what *TOTP* was – *The Mousetrap* of music TV.'

Tony Christie, looking not at all like a quiz show host.

Don't Give Up On Us, Dave Lee

The curtain came down on *TOTP* with a special final edition on Sunday 30 July 2006 and, fittingly, its filming had to be shaped around the quixotic lifestyle of Sir Jimmy Savile.

Savile had for 34 years been the honorary chieftain of the Lochaber Highland Games in Scotland, an event he attended annually in a tartan tracksuit. As it was scheduled for the same day and he declined to break with his personal tradition, *TOTP*'s swansong was pre-recorded four days earlier.

Presenters reappeared from every era of the show's history, with old-timers Savile, Tony Blackburn, Dave Lee

> ## 'What did I think? I thought "Wow, that was something else, baby!"'
>
> **Sir Jimmy Savile**

Travis, Mike Read, Janice Long and Pat Sharp being joined by the new blood of Sarah Cawood, Rufus Hound, Edith Bowman and Reggie Yates.

However, Yates's regular co-host during the show's demise, Fearne Cotton, was absent from the auspicious occasion, preferring to fly to Fiji to film ITV1's *Love Island*.

The nostalgia-fest programme ranged far and wide through *TOTP*'s illustrious 42-year history, with the 1960s represented by archive monochrome footage of the Rolling Stones, Supremes, Righteous Brothers, Stevie Wonder, Tom Jones and the Hollies.

From the 1970s, Slade, Queen, Mud, Bob Marley, Abba, John Lennon, the Three

An eighties revival: Mike Read and Pat Sharp.

Degrees and Blondie led up to a film of Michael Jackson's sole *TOTP* appearance, in 1972, aged 14, sporting a red-and-yellow jumpsuit and a proud Afro for 'Rockin' Robin'.

A novelty records sequence revisited Clive Dunn, St Winifred's School Choir, the Wombles, the Smurfs, the Tweets and the Crazy Frog, with a glimpse of a mock-choked John Peel: 'This is a very important moment in my life: here are Keith Harris and Orville.'

Spandau Ballet, Duran Duran, Adam & the Ants, Bros and Madonna were among the artists representing the 1980s, while footage of Oasis, Blur, Take That, Nirvana, Prince and Robbie Williams stood for the following decade.

Britney, Girls Aloud, 50 Cent, Eminem, Gnarls Barkley and James Blunt brought the story up to date but, as ever with *TOTP*, the bits between the songs were equally telling.

The love-it-or-loathe-it zany humour of the show's golden era made a reappearance, with Tony Blackburn bizarrely claiming that David Bowie's groundbreaking 1972 'Starman' image was 'based entirely on me, actually!'

The multicoloured-waistcoat-sporting DLT was in his element, stealing a kiss from the demure Babs of Pan's People and claiming to have solved the mystery of what the Spice Girls meant by zigazig-ah: 'They're what Jimmy smokes, aren't they? Ha ha!'

The programme inevitably adopted its habitual mode of hail-fellow-well-met boisterousness, but underpinning the forced jollity was an ineffable mood of sadness.

'That's true, but I loved doing the last show more than any other one I had done,' muses Tony Blackburn. 'We were all so much older and got on so much better.

'My favourite moment was when Mike Read had to do an

Tony Blackburn bemoans the absence of Simon Bates.

introduction which involved him climbing a stepladder and this young assistant asked him, "Do you need any help getting up there?" Mike said to me, "Oh God, you heard that, didn't you?"'

After a video of that week's No. 1, Shakira's 'Hips Don't Lie', the farewell *TOTP* climaxed with Sir Jimmy Savile ducking behind a curtain, turning off the studio lights and wandering off shaking his head, an unlit cigar in his mouth.

'It was an historic moment,' notes Mike Read. 'Jimmy is as mad as a box of frogs but I'm a very emotional, spiritual person, and when he switched off the lights and shuffled off, I found that very touching.'

With typical perversity, however, Savile declared himself utterly unmoved by the death of *TOTP*.

'I didn't feel emotional at all, I thought it was terrific,' he reflects. 'It just made me realise that I had invented the show in 1964 and I closed it down 42 years later.

'What did I think? I thought, "Wow, that was something else, baby!"'

So much accumulated wisdom on one tiny stage.

Back For Good?

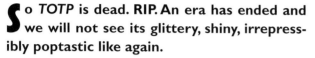

So *TOTP* is dead. RIP. An era has ended and we will not see its glittery, shiny, irrepressibly poptastic like again.

Or will we?

After the BBC pulled the plug on *TOTP* in 2006, a host of influential figures from its illustrious past queued up to condemn the move. Noel Edmonds, the pioneer who gave the nation the dual Reithian totems of Mr Blobby and *Deal Or No Deal*, was scathing.

'It's dangerous to throw out one of the most recognised brands in TV today,' he declaimed. 'Kids are still listening to music. It's a tragedy when a broadcaster doesn't understand such a powerful brand.'

Yet despite the show's demise, the *TOTP* brand has not evaporated. The glossy *Smash Hits*-style spin-off magazine is still going strong (which is more than can be said for *Smash Hits*). On TV, *TOTP2* gets good ratings figures and now features fresh live performances.

Of course, *TOTP* would be bucking a trend were it to return. None of the main UK terrestrial networks now runs a peak-time music show. Even the music-focused kids' TV shows on Saturday mornings have been scaled back.

The days of the family gathering around the TV to count down the hit parade are no more: 'The idea today of watching a pop show with your grandma is unthinkable,' notes David Jensen.

Status Quo appeared on *TOTP* more times than anybody...

Nevertheless, some feel the eventual return of the seminal show is inevitable.

'TOTP absolutely will come back,' reckons Johnny Marr. 'It won't be exactly like it was, but the BBC will realise it was a huge mistake to take it off.'

The BBC, of course, has previous form in killing off iconic programmes only to resurrect them. In 1989, it brought the axe down on the long-running Saturday night sci-fi series *Dr Who* after 26 years, before reinventing a sharper, better take on the format in 2005.

So could there be a way for a more lithe, fitter *TOTP* to adapt and survive for the 21st century?

Yes, says Keith Mullen, once the guitarist in The Farm but now a lecturer at the Liverpool Institute for the

> ## 'Young people will always love watching music. If they went back to the original *TOTP*, it would be a belter.'
>
> ### Sir Jimmy Savile

Performing Arts: 'I've been telling my students to make their own *TOTP* and put it on YouTube. *TOTP* needs to go underground.'

Yet such a venture would inevitably be marginal. It's more telling that *TOTP*'s oldest hands, steeped in the politics and machinations of the BBC, feel the show is bound to return — and probably sooner rather than later.

'*TOTP* is too good a brand not to come back,' reflects Dave Lee Travis. 'In a couple of years people will have forgotten about the bad things of the last few years, focus on what was great earlier on and want to see it again.'

'I would love, love, *love* to be given *TOTP*, because I know I could get it back up there and make it a hugely popular programme,' avers Mike Read.

'It could have some tracks from outside the chart, a download chart, album tracks, greatest hits and maybe even a pop quiz. If I were allowed to make a genuine music programme like that, I would guarantee the BBC five million viewers a week.'

Yet the strongest declaration of faith in the magic and mystery of *TOTP* comes from the King Solomon of pop, who invented it in a converted Manchester church 43 years ago.

'They just need to go back to square one,' concludes Sir Jimmy Savile. 'Young people will always love watching music. If they went back to the original *TOTP*, it would be a belter.'

... except Sir Cliff Richard. So that was OK.

The Toppermost of the Poppermost

This book would not have been possible without the memories of the following pop pickers, to whom I am hugely grateful…
Frank Allen, Marc Almond, Cheryl Baker, Tommy Banner, Dave Bartram, Cilla Black, Jet Black, Tony Blackburn, Ric Blaxill, Colin Blunstone, Clint Boon, Billy Bragg, Yasmin Bucknor, Tony Christie, Flick Colby, Dave Cousins, Lynsey de Paul, Bobby Elliott, Richard Fairbrass, Nigel Fletcher, David Gedge, Colin Gibb, Danny Goffey, Graham Gouldman, Glenn Gregory, David Hamilton, Fran Healy, Bob Henrit, Noddy Holder, Tony Horkins, Englebert Humperdinck, Wayne Hussey, Clive Jackson, David Jacobs, David 'Kid' Jensen, Samantha Juste, Gary Kemp, Katrina Leskanich, Sally Lindsay, Guy Lloyd, Meat Loaf, Janice Long, Eddie Lundon, Ron Mael, Maggot, Johnny Marr, Andy McCluskey, Ian McCulloch, Mark Morriss, Keith Mullen, Pete Murray, Mike Nolan, Peter Noone, Gary Numan, William Orbit, Donny Osmond, Andi Peters, Brian Poole, Babs Powell, Reg Presley, Shelley Preston, Mike Read, Craig Reid, Sir Cliff Richard, Emperor Rosko, Francis Rossi, Sean Rowley, Phill Savidge, Sir Jimmy Savile, Rat Scabies, Johnny Sharp, Jeff Simpson, Bob Stanley, Nicky Stevens, Nick Tesco, Glenn Tilbrook, Dave Lee Travis, Diane White, Robert Wyatt.

Like *TOTP*, we may well return. Have you appeared on *TOTP*, as an artist, technician or audience member? Please email **totp@btinternet.com**